W0254406

The Collected Works of Caravan of Dreams Theater

Gilgamesh - Marouf the Cobbler - Faust, Part One

Billy the Kid - Metal Woman - Tin Can Man

Life Is A Dream - Don Juan - The Brothers Karamazov

Napoleon Jones - The Energy Empire
Empire of the Night - Deconstruction of the Countdown

Tamarand - The Guru - McNeckel's Folly

Prometheus Bound - Oedipus Tyrannos
Oedipus at Colonus

Socrates - Shakespeare and Fitton - Siegfried's Death

THE COLLECTED WORKS OF

CARAVAN OF DREAMS THEATER

VOLUME I

GILGAMESH

MAROUF THE COBBLER

FAUST Part One

SYNERGETIC PRESS

First Edition, 1983

Published by Synergetic Press
24 Old Gloucester Street, London WC1

ISBN 0 907791 01 8

Printed in Great Britain by Express Litho Service, Oxford

CONTENTS

To Tambimuttu

INTRODUCTION

Caravan of Dreams Theater, an international actors' ensemble, was conceived in San Francisco in 1967 with the objective of forming a troupe to portray the essence of historical epochs, After working for a year in New York City and Houston, Texas, the ensemble established a permanent base near Santa Fe, New Mexico in 1969. Since that time, Caravan has produced three North American theater tours and eleven intercontinental tours with performances in England, Europe, Asia, Australia, North and South America.[1]

This series of seven volumes reflects the historical focus of Caravan's work and includes dramatizations, adaptations and new translations of existing plays, literary works and traditional legends, as well as original works of a contemporary nature.

This volume, the first in the series, commences with the first recorded text containing the scenes and throughline of drama, *Gilgamesh.* Written, some scholars maintain, as early as the fourth millennium B.C., the epic of *Gilgamesh* introduced the 'conquest of nature' theme whose consequences are being widely realized only now in the latter part of the 20th century. *Marouf the Cobbler* originates from another ancient Middle Eastern tradition, passed on in oral and written form throughout the centuries and presented to the West in the *Thousand and One Nights.* Preserving the poetry of Sir Richard Burton's translation, Caravan's *Marouf* deals with the magical consequences of changes in location, a theme profoundly integrated in Western culture. Goethe's *Faust, Part One* – the modern epic of the individual seeking cosmic power for personal enlightenment; the tragedy of Faust of Western Civilization who, in despair of finding truth, sells his soul for power over existence; or, from another perspective, the tragedy of Margareta who falls unknowing in the maelstrom of Faust's limitless aspirations – is a multi-faceted mythology laying bare the force of contradictions of the Western dynamic toward infinity.

[1] Caravan of Dreams Theater went under the name of Theater of All Possibilities from 1967 to 1983. See also, *Theater of All Possibilities* (Editions Poetry London, London, 1980).

GILGAMESH

Adapted from a Caravan of Dreams Theater collation of the Sumerian, Akkadian and Hittite Englished texts.

CHARACTERS

GILGAMESH
PEOPLE
TEMPLE DANCERS
TRAPPER
NIMSUN
ENKIDU
HUMBABA
ISHTAR
EA
BULL OF HEAVEN
ENLIL
SHEMS
KEEPER OF THE BOOK OF DEATH
SCORPIONS
SIDURI
URSHUNABI
UTNAPISHTIM
WOMAN
SERPENT

Scene 1

(Street in Uruk. People watch two gamblers rolling dice.)

PEOPLE
(Chant)
Gilgamesh, King of Uruk
Two thirds god, one third man
He works the people dawn to dusk
To build the seven walls planned by seven sages
long forgotten
He pays out our young men's lives
Gaining glory in his wars
He takes each maiden that he wishes
First in beauty, first in courage
Strong as a wild bull
Arrogant beyond measure
Who can fight him as an equal
And remove his burden from our backs?

Scene 2

(Gilgamesh striding in his palace, a temple dancer attends him.)

GILGAMESH
They complain?

DANCER
I don't.

GILGAMESH
They don't understand that all their work so far is nothing, nothing compared to –

DANCER
Compared to –

GILGAMESH
Don't mock me or I'll have you thrown out of the Temple, into the street.

DANCER
I want to understand you.

GILGAMESH
You can't understand me. Nobody here in Uruk understands me. Let me build this little City into a jewel, some dog will plunder it, burn it to the ground within a century; let me win a war, my successor will lose and the enemy will rewrite history; let me love all the girls one night apiece, they'll forget after a thousand nights with someone else.

TRAPPER
(Enters) Gilgamesh, my father sends me to you. A wild man who lives with the animals, stronger than any man, breaks into our traps, sets the animals free, breaks up our hunting parties, destroys our dogs. My father says, "Ask Gilgamesh to send to us a temple dancer, let her make love to this monster, half-man, half-beast, let her wait for him by the spring, make love to him, and the animals will reject him."

GILGAMESH
Take this girl. Go with him. Tame the animal. Leave me alone with my thoughts. *(Trapper and temple dancer leave.)*

Scene 3

(Spring. Dancer and trapper wait.)

DANCER
We've waited here at this spring for three days and no animals have come. Do you really know what you're talking about?

TRAPPER
You need patience in the wilderness.

DANCER
In the City we become bored, forget and seek new sensations.

TRAPPER
There come the animals! There's the wild man with them. Now, don't get embarrassed, don't dilly-dally, go right for him, open to him, welcome him. Take off your clothes, let him look at you, take you. When he touches you, embrace him, lie with him. Teach this untamed savage man the lover's art, because after he has been with you, the animals that have let him share their life will then reject him.

DANCER
I will. Leave now, I will bring him to you. *(She calls to Enkidu, singing him to her. She dances before him, slowly removing her garments. He stands rapt. She pulls him to the ground. Lights down. On the other side of the stage lights up; Gilgamesh talking to his mother, Nimsun.)*

GILGAMESH
Last night I dreamed. Joy overflowed from me, the young men thronged about me, I strode through the night beneath the stars. Then a meteor flashed through the skies, fell at my feet. I tried to pick it up, too heavy. All the people in Uruk ran to see it, young and old, men and women. They admired and kissed it. It attracted me like a woman and I grew jealous. The young men helped me. I braced my shoulders, lifted it, brought it to you. You pronounced it my brother.

NIMSUN
What you saw, what attracted you like a woman, this meteor, was the strong comrade, he who *helps* his friend. Strongest of all the animals, born in the grasslands, rover of mountains, he will gladden your heart; he is as strong as you. *(Lights down. Lights up on other side of stage.)*

ENKIDU
(Returning to dancer.) For six days and seven nights we did it. But I had enough. I left you to run again with the animals. They ran away from me, they snorted, whinnied, reared up against me. I ran after them. My knees buckled from weakness. They disappeared in dust. What have you done to me?

DANCER
Why do you still want to act like an animal? You are now thinking like a human being, not like them. You are now like Gilgamesh, like a god; the Temple of Ishtar, goddess of love, will open to you, the walls of Uruk receive you . . .

ENKIDU
Gilgamesh . . . god . . . love . . . walls of Uruk . . .

DANCER
Gilgamesh is strongest. He pushes the City beyond endurance.

ENKIDU
I will go fight Gilgamesh. I will challenge his right to rule. I will cry aloud, I am the strongest. Lead me to this walled City, to this Temple of Love, I will change the order of things. *(Lights down. Lights up on other side of stage.)*

GILGAMESH
Mother, I have dreamed a second dream. In the center of Uruk gleamed an axe, strangely shaped. Young and old, men and women, thronged about kissing it. I loved it like a woman, grew jealous, took it and wore it at my side.

NIMSUN
That axe, which attracted you with the power of the love of a woman, that axe is the strong friend that I will give you. He will arrive in his strength, as strong as you, the brave companion who rescues his friend. *(Lights down. Lights up on other side of the stage.)*

DANCER
Let me dress you with part of my scarlet robe. Now learn to eat bread, it is our food. Drink wine, it is our custom. I will wash you with perfume and oil and comb your hair while you drink.

TRAPPER
(Enters) Instead of our robber you have become our protector. You stand watch at night against the lions and wolves. You're lucky to be here, there's another uproar in Uruk; Gilgamesh insists upon his right and will take another virgin tonight while the drums roll, and her chosen man and family must sit by until he finishes with her. The City groans but no one dares to fight him.

ENKIDU
I will go now. I will stop him.

Scene 4

(Enkidu strides into Uruk, accompanied by the dancer and the trapper.)

PEOPLE ONE
Look, at last Gilgamesh will meet his match!

PEOPLE TWO
Almost the spitting image of him!

PEOPLE THREE
This one was reared on the milk of wild beasts. He's stronger.

ALL
Hail Enkidu! *(Drums; Gilgamesh enters at head of procession.)*

ENKIDU
You're not going to get this virgin.

(People cheer Enkidu. Gilgamesh strides up to him and attacks. They fight. Wolfishly, tigerishly, bellow like bulls, gasp like horses. The people shriek. Gilgamesh finally stands still, exhausted. Enkidu has just strength enough to push him. They look at each other, then burst into laughter and embrace.)

Scene 5

GILGAMESH
I love adventure. Enkidu, we go together into the mountains, cut down one of the cedars in the sacred forest of the gods, and kill the evil one, Humbaba.

ENKIDU
Uu-uuh.

GILGAMESH
Why do you groan? Let's be off.

ENKIDU
I'm afraid.

GILGAMESH
Didn't we promise to stick together forever no matter what obstacle came up?

ENKIDU
All right. But my heart is sick
The sound of sorrow hoarsens my throat,
My arms feel like they're hollow.

GILGAMESH
Humbaba has taken your strength,
We have to kill him,
End his evil power.

ENKIDU
No, this adventure will cost our life.

GILGAMESH
Why should we be afraid?
When we are together?
Even of Humbaba, the Ferocious.
How can we cut down and carry out that cedar?

ENKIDU
When I ran with the animals,
We discovered that forest.
It is ten thousand leagues size
In all directions.
Humbaba guards it,
A terror to flesh.
His roar is the flood,
His breath the forest fire,
His jaws are death.
When a twig rustles beneath an insect
Humbaba hears it sixty miles away,
Twitches and the bug dies.
Who would go willingly into that forest,
Explore its darkness?
Weakness creeps into all who enter,
Humbaba never sleeps,
The struggle is unequal, Gilgamesh.

GILGAMESH
Show me a man who can fly to Heaven!
Only the gods live forever
Companions to the glorious Sun,
But the days of us men are numbered,
Our projects but gusts of wind,
So fear is never rational.
Well, if you're afraid,
I'll go first, you can call out:

Go on, and if I die
Men will say
He died fighting
The fierce Humbaba.
You can't discourage me
With your hesitations.
I will fight Humbaba.
I will cut down his cedar.

Scene 6

(Nïmsun accompanied by two temple dancers; Gilgamesh, Enkidu enter.)

GILGAMESH
Mother, the counsellors of the City moan at Enkidu and me. They say you are young, foolhardy, you don't understand what going to seek out Humbaba means.

NIMSUN
You are going to attack Humbaba?

GILGAMESH
They say
Humbaba does not die like men
His weapons are invincible
His roar is like flood
His breath like the forest fire
His jaws are death.
Why do you wish to do this, Gilgamesh
Humbaba does not fight fairly.

ENKIDU
Gilgamesh answered,
He laughed at the counsellors

He asked me,
Shall I answer that I am afraid of Humbaba
That I shall be a stay-at-home
Fat and afraid as these men?

GILGAMESH
I said we shall go to Nimsun
Nimsun the Queen knows the deep knowledge,
She must give us counsel.
Now, Nimsun, listen to me;
I must travel a long journey,
To the Forest of Humbaba,
To fight no common fight.

NIMSUN
(Putting on her finest costume, lighting incense.)
O Sun,
Why did you give this restless heart
To Gilgamesh, my son, why?
Now he sets out on a long journey,
To the Forest of Humbaba,
On an unknown road
To fight no common fight.
So from the moment he leaves,
Until he reaches the Forest of Cedars,
Until he kills Humbaba,
O Sun, do not forget him;
Let the dawn remind you daily,
Give him sleep each night.
(She puts out incense.)
Enkidu,
You are not my body's child,
But you shall be like my child.
(Places amulet around his neck.)
I trust my son with you.
Bring him back safely.
(They leave.)

Scene 7

(Before the great door of Humbaba.)

GILGAMESH
We have made six weeks journey
In three days. Here is the
Door to Humbaba's forest.
Suddenly I feel afraid.

ENKIDU
Gilgamesh, remember
Your bragging in Uruk.
Forward, what do we have to fear?

GILGAMESH
Yes, let's move right in.
Don't let Humbaba escape into the forest.
He's not had time
To put on more than one
Of his seven suits of armor.
(Humbaba roars within.)

ENKIDU
(Charges gates with axe upraised.)
It's too beautiful to shatter!
(Puts down his axe, opens with his hand.)
Ay! Gilgamesh, don't go into the forest,
When I opened the gate
My hand's paralysed!

GILGAMESH
Don't talk like a coward.
Did we overcome so many dangers,
Travel so far on an unknown road,
Only to turn back as soon as we arrive?
Keep close to me now,

You will use your hand again.
Would my friend stay behind?
No, we go together
Into the heart of the forest.
Rouse up your courage
Thinking of the fight ahead of us;
Forget death and follow me,
A brave man but not a fool.
When two friends fight together,
Each protects the other.
If they die, their name lives on.
(They advance into forest.)

Scene 8

(Gilgamesh, Enkidu sleeping. Gilgamesh starts awake.)

GILGAMESH
Enkidu, did you wake me up?
Enkidu!

ENKIDU
What?

GILGAMESH
My friend, I dreamed a dream.
We travelled a deep gorge,
A landslide just missed us,
We were like two bugs beside it.
Then I dreamed a second dream.
The landslide fell again,
Knocked my feet out from under me,
A blazing light,
And in the light
Stood one of grace and beauty

Far beyond this world's beauty.
He pulled me out,
Gave me water,
Restored my courage,
And lifted me to my feet.

ENKIDU
That dream is good, excellent.
That landslide is Humbaba.
Even if he falls on us with all his force,
We shall win!

GILGAMESH
Now you have a dream!
(They go back to sleep.)

ENKIDU
Did you call me?
If not, it must have been my dream.
The sky thundered,
The earth tremored,
Darkness, lightning, forest fire,
Clouds lowering, raining death.
Suddenly the lightning stopped glaring,
The fire burnt out,
The sparks became ashes.
What does this mean, Gilgamesh?

GILGAMESH
Who can say?

ENKIDU
You don't want to say.

GILGAMESH
Come on. Let's go after Humbaba.
(They leave.)

Scene 9

GILGAMESH
(Grasping his axe.)
We're deep into the forest.
I'll chop down a cedar tree.
(Swings away.)
I'm growing weak, sleepy.

ENKIDU
Gilgamesh!
Don't force your mother into mourning!

GILGAMESH
By the life of Nimsun, my mother,
And by my divine father,
Until I fight Humbaba
I will not turn back to the City.

ENKIDU
You don't know this monster,
That's why you seem so brave.
I know him, I am terrified.
His teeth are demon's fangs,
His expression like a lion,
He charges with the flood,
Crushing trees and reeds.
Go on if you desire,
I will go back to the City.
I will tell your mother
Of your glorious deeds
Till she shouts with joy,
Then I will tell of your death,
And she will weep with bitterness.

GILGAMESH
Fire and sacrifice aren't for me yet
The boat of the dead will not set sail,

They won't stitch my shroud,
My people will not mourn yet,
They will not burn my house,
Nor light my pyre.
Give me your help today,
And I will give you mine,
What can go wrong?
All creatures born of flesh
Sail at last in the boat to the West,
And when it sinks, they are gone,
But you and I shall go forward,
And face Humbaba eye-to-eye.
If you are afraid, throw fear away.
If you are terrified, throw terror away.
Take up your axe, let's attack.
He who doesn't finish a fight
He's started knows no peace.

(Humbaba rushes at them, roars, growls.)

GILGAMESH
Help me now, O Sun!

(Humbaba attacks them, beating them back. Enkidu falls. The Four Winds blow against Humbaba, blinding his eye. Gilgamesh and Enkidu prevail against him.)

HUMBABA
Don't kill me. Don't kill me.
I'll serve you like the gods.
I'll build you a palace with my cedars.

GILGAMESH
Enkidu
Why shouldn't he return to his forest,
The captive to his mother?

ENKIDU
The strongest man falls to fate
If he has no judgment.
If you let him loose again in his forest,
My friend will never
Return to his mother.
He will block the mountain path.

HUMBABA
Enkidu, you speak evil:
Afraid of a rival in your friendship,
You speak evil.

ENKIDU
Don't listen, Gilgamesh. Humbaba must die!

GILGAMESH
If we kill him,
The glory and glamor
Of his forest will be destroyed.

ENKIDU
No, indeed, my friend,
First trap the mother bird
Where will the chicks run to?
Afterwards we shall gain
The glory and glamor.

(With three strokes Gilgamesh chops off Humbaba's head. He reaches out to Enkidu's wounded back.)

Scene 10

(Gilgamesh finishing dressing himself in his finest robes. Ishtar appears at his side, admiring him.)

ISHTAR

Gilgamesh, come, be my lover.
Give me the seed of your sex.
Let me be yours and you be mine.
I will give you a swift chariot
Of malachite and wheels of gold,
With horns of copper;
Storm demons will act as your horses;
Our house fragrant, built of cedarwood;
Kings, princes, rulers will bow to you,
Send you tribute of mountains, plain and sea.
Your ewes will drop twins,
Your she-goats triplets,
Your pack-ass outrun race-horses,
Your chariot horses swiftest upon earth.

GILGAMESH

This you speak of giving me, Ishtar.
What would you want in return?
What ointments would a goddess wish?
What perfumes, what weave for an immortal?
And even so, if I did take you as lover,
What would happen to me?
Your lovers have found you
To be a brazier that smokes and smoulders in the cold,
A backdoor that can't keep out wind or storm,
A temple crashing down on the heads of its worshippers,
Tar that sticks to the hand trying to use it,
A leaky wineskin that soddens the bearer,
A sandal that trips the runner.
Which of your lovers do you love forever?
What mortal pleases you more than briefly?

ISHTAR

Oooh!

GILGAMESH

Listen, while I tell what happened to your lovers.

Tammuz, the lover of your girlhood,
You have ordered his endless wailing,
Men mourn his fate;
He who comes to you, a gorgeous bird,
You strike and break his wings;
He who comes to you like a lion,
You dig seven pits for him, and seven more;
He who comes to you a glorious stallion,
Magnificent for battle, you whip and spur
Till tired out he drinks muddy water;
He who comes to you a proud shepherd,
You turn into a wolf,
Stoned by his boys, bitten by his dogs.
And what about your father's gardener?
Every day he brought you delicious dates.
You turned your eyes on him,
You said, dearest Ishullann,
Come here, let me enjoy your manhood,
Come here, take me, I am yours.
Ishullann refused.
You struck him, changed him into a blind mole,
Digging in the earth,
His desire always beyond his reach.
And if I became your lover
Wouldn't you treat me like all the rest
That you picked up, briefly loved, then crushed?

ISHTAR

Your insolence will cost you your life . . .
(Leaves)

Scene 11

(Ishtar and Ea.)

ISHTAR
Father, Gilgamesh insulted me,
He spoke aloud all about
My lurid behavior, my disgraceful deeds.

EA
You brought it on yourself.
Because of your own behavior,
Gilgamesh spoke aloud all about
Your lurid behavior, your disgraceful deeds.

ISHTAR
Father, make me the Bull of Heaven
And let him destroy Gilgamesh.
Fill Gilgamesh with arrogance,
Let him bring on his own destruction!
If you refuse to make the Bull of Heaven for me,
I will break down the doors of Hell,
Turn all the dead loose,
They will all arise, outnumber the living
And eat up all their food.

EA
If I make the Bull of Heaven as you desire,
There will be seven years of drought,
The wheat will be seedless husks.
Have you put up enough grain for men,
Enough fodder for the cattle?
Men need to survive their punishments.

ISHTAR
I have put by grain for men,
Fodder for the cattle;
There's enough for them to get by for seven years.

EA

I will do it.

Scene 12

(Enkidu and Gilgamesh with axes seeking the Bull of Heaven. They encounter him.)

ENKIDU

You refused Ishtar.
She has sent the Bull of Heaven.
With his first snort he killed a hundred men,
And then another hundred, and another.
With his second snort he killed
Three hundred men.
Now with his third snort
He will try to kill me.
(Enkidu catches the Bull by the horns.)
My friend we boasted
We wanted to leave names behind,
Thrust in your sword
Between the neck and horns!
(Gilgamesh kills the Bull.)

GILGAMESH

Now we shall sacrifice his heart
To the glorious Sun!

ISHTAR

Woe to Gilgamesh
Who scorned me by killing the Bull of Heaven!

ENKIDU

(Throwing her a hunk of meat cut off from the Bull.)

If I could lay my hands on you,
I'd cut a piece out of you!
(They leave.)

(Ishtar calls in two of her temple dancing girls and they mourn the Bull.)

(Offstage shouts:)

Who is the most glorious of men?
Who is the greatest of men?
Gilgamesh! Gilgamesh!

Scene 13

(Enkidu sleeping; Ishtar, Ea, Enlil.)

ISHTAR

One of them at least must die!
They both should die
For the killing of Humbaba
And the killing of the Bull of Heaven.
But at least one must die!

EA

I think
Gilgamesh is the most guilty;
Not only did he do the actual killings
But he chopped down the great cedar.

ENLIL

Gilgamesh?
Enkidu is the real criminal.
He showed Gilgamesh the way
To the Forest of the Cedars!

EA

What right have you to speak?
You hurled the winds at Humbaba,
Blinding him in his battle.

ENLIL
What about you?
And what about you?
Without you,
Neither would have dared to do these things!
You encouraged them
Giving special dreams
Coming to their help!

ISHTAR
What's the use of arguing
Which of us is guilty?
One of them must die,
I'll settle for that.
Which shall it be?
(Lights fade from the gods to go up on Enkidu.)

ENKIDU
Gilgamesh!

GILGAMESH
(Entering)
What is it?

ENKIDU
I have dreamed a dream.
The gods were arguing
As to which of us
Would have to die
For killing Humbaba and the Bull of Heaven.
My dream ended before they decided,
But I know that I am doomed.

GILGAMESH
You have a fever.

ENKIDU
No, this was a true vision.

GILGAMESH
My friend, my comrade,
Do the gods imagine that by killing you
They will let me go free?
No, my friend,
I shall kneel like a beggar
For all of my days
Upon the threshold of death,
Waiting for his door to open,
So that I can enter and see your face!
(Leaves)

ENKIDU
I roamed the mountains,
Carefree, friends with the animals,
The sun, the winds, the rivers,
And then that girl found me,
Pulled me to the ground, took my strength,
Lured me to the City of men,
I went adventuring toward the forest,
The beautiful door paralyzed my hand
When I tried to open it!
I curse that girl,
I curse those men,
I curse that door,
How I wish it had never happened!

(A ray of sunlight and Shems appears, and dancing girl pantomimes her drama with Enkidu.)

SHEMS
Enkidu, not all of your life
Among men has been dark,
And why are you cursing the girl
Who taught you to eat bread fit for gods
And drink wine vatted for kings?
Who dressed you in magnificent garments,
And gave you Gilgamesh for friend,

Gilgamesh, your true brother,
Who has given you a royal bed,
And a couch to recline on at his left hand?
He has made the noble of the earth kiss your feet,
The men of Uruk will lament and wail over you.
When you are dead,
He will grow his hair long in your memory,
He will wear only a lion's skin,
He will wander in the desert.

ENKIDU
I will call back my curse.
Let no man scorn the dancing girl,
Striking his thigh in ridicule.
Kings, princes, rulers shall love you,
The old man waggle his beard,
The young man undo his belt.
For you gold, carnelian and malachite
Will be heaped in the strong-room.
For you, the wife
The mother of seven shall be forsaken.
The priests shall make way before you
Into the presence of the gods.
(He sleeps. A toad, Keeper of the Book of Death, enters, squats, glowers at Enkidu. Gilgamesh enters, watches over him.)
I dreamed a dream again, my friend.
The skies thundered and cried out,
A frightening being, lion-faced,
Swooped on me like an eagle of the black storm,
His talons pierced my back;
As he carried me off,
My arms sprouted feathers,
I became like him!
His eyes burned into mine,
And I knew I was being carried
Into the house from which no one who enters
comes out again,

Down the road of no return.
In that house kings, priests, nobles,
  all huddle in blackness,
Eating dirt and dust instead of bread and meat,
The Keeper of the Book of Death squatted there,
Raised her eyes, saw me, and said,
"Who brought this one?"
Here, feel my heart pounding with terror.

GILGAMESH

Who in this great City
Has wisdom like this?
You speak strange things
Why do you speak so strangely?
The dream was extraordinary,
The terror overpowering.
We must value the dream,
No matter what the terror;
Because the dream has shown
Misery comes at the last to the healthy man,
That the end of life is sorrow.

ENKIDU

My friend, the goddess of love and war
Cursed me and I must die this shameful death.
I shall not die in battle;
I feared that,
But happy the man dying in battle,
I must die like this in bed.
(Enkidu dies.)

GILGAMESH

Enkidu,
The deer, the gazelle, the stags weep for you,
The paths that you loved
In the forests murmur for you,
You were the axe at my side,
The bow in my hand,

The knife in my belt,
My shield, my robe,
My delight!
You and I braved and endured everything,
Scaled the mountains,
Hunted the leopard!
You and I fought Humbaba of the dark forest
And grappled the Bull of Heaven!
Now, behold,
Shrouded in darkness,
You cannot hear my voice!
(Gilgamesh veils Enkidu's face, tears off his garments, roars like a lioness robbed of her whelps.)
Now I have seen the face of death,
I am afraid.
One day I too shall be like Enkidu.

Scene 14

GILGAMESH
(Dancing girl prepares Gilgamesh. Dressed in lionskin, he roams the wilderness.)
There is no rest, no peace, despair.
What my friend is, that shall I be.
I am afraid of death.
(Lion enters, fights. Gilgamesh beheads lion.)
I shall go to Utnapishtim, the Faraway,
The only man on earth who has escaped death,
Whom the gods rescued from the Flood,
And set to live in the Garden of the Sun.
I shall learn from him
The secret of eternal life.

(Two scorpions rise menacingly. Gilgamesh recoils, then advances forward.)

FIRST SCORPION
This man who keeps approaching,
He must be a god.

SECOND SCORPION
Two thirds. But one third is man.

FIRST SCORPION
Why have you come on this long journey?
For what have you travelled so far,
Crossing dangerous deserts and seas?

GILGAMESH
I am on the way to my teacher,
Utnapishtim.
I dearly loved my friend Enkidu,
We endured many hardships together,
I come on his behalf,
For the common fate of man has taken him.
I have wept for him,
I would not let them take his body,
I hoped he would come back because of my weeping.
Since he left, I count my life as nothing;
This is why I journey here,
Searching for Utnapishtim, my teacher;
For men say he lives in the Garden of the Sun
And has found eternal life.
I wish to question him about life and death.

FIRST SCORPION
No man born of woman has done this,
No mortal has passed this mountain;
It is twelve leagues long of darkness;
There is no light.

GILGAMESH
Be it never so long,
And never so dark,

Be the pains and dangers never so great,
Be the heat never so searing,
The cold never so bitter,
I am resolved to go this way.

FIRST SCORPION
Go, Gilgamesh, we permit you
To pass the mountain of Mashu,
Through the high ranges.
May your feet carry you safely home.
The gate of the mountain opens for you.

Scene 15

GILGAMESH
I have walked for a day in this darkness,
Will I never come to the end?
(Light)
I have made it through the mountain
Through thirteen leagues of darkness
This must be the Garden of the Sun
Fruits of carnelian,
Leaves of malachite,
Thorns of hematite,
Pebbles of pearl!
Light everywhere!

SHEMS
(Appears)
Enjoy the garden. Stop!
Never has mortal man been allowed so far.
Nor will another so long as winds make waves.
That immortal life for which you search
You will never find.

GILGAMESH

Now that I have labored and struggled
So far through the wilderness,
Should I go to sleep,
Let the earth cover me forever?
I will not forget my purpose,
I remember Enkidu,
Let my eyes see sunlight,
Until they blink dazzled with overlooking.
Though I be no better than a dead man,
Still give me the light of the sun!

SIDURI

(Enters, sings.)

I live beside the sea,
I am the woman of the vine,
I am the maker of the wine.
(Sees Gilgamesh.)
Surely this is some criminal.
Where is he going to?
His cheeks are starved,
His face is drawn,
Despair is in his heart.

GILGAMESH

Why shouldn't my cheeks be starved,
My face drawn, my heart in despair?
My face has travelled far,
Exposed to heat and cold.
I wander the wilderness of the world
In search of my friend.
My friend, whom I hunted the leopard with,
Who fought together with me
Against Humbaba and the Bull of Heaven,
Enkidu, my brother, the one I loved,
The end of mortal life came to him.
I mourned over him for seven days and nights
Until the worm entered him.

Because of my friend I fear death,
Because of my friend
I search the world's wilderness and cannot rest.
And now, girl, maker of the wine,
Now that I have seen your face,
Do not let me see the face of death
Which I dread.

SIDURI

Gilgamesh, why do you hurry
  through the world's wilderness?
You will never find that immortal life
For which you search.
When the gods created man,
They gave him for his portion death,
But life they kept for themselves.
So, Gilgamesh, fill your belly with good things,
Day and night, night and day.
Dance, make merry, feast, rejoice.
Let your clothes be cool and fresh,
Bathe yourself in clean water,
Cherish the little child holding your hand,
Make your woman happy in your embrace,
This, too, is the portion given to man.

GILGAMESH

How can I stop, how can I rest,
When Enkidu whom I love is turned to dust,
And I too shall die
And be laid away in the dirt forever?

SIDURI

Let me rub your back. Relax.
Stay here. I will love you.
Enjoy wine in the garden of the gods.

GILGAMESH

Girl, tell me, now,

What is the way to Utnapishtim?
What are the directions?
Give me, please give me the directions.
I will cross the ocean if I have to,
And if it is possible,
Or I will wander further into the world's wilderness.

SIDURI

Gilgamesh, there is no crossing that ocean.
Whoever arrived here, since the first days,
Has never been able to pass that sea.
The sun alone crosses it.
The waters of death flow deep within it.
Gilgamesh, how can you cross that ocean?
When you face the waters of death, what could you do?

GILGAMESH

Tell me, please tell me.

SIDURI

Gilgamesh, down in the reeds
You can find Urshunabi,
The ferryman of Utnapishtim,
Around him are the stones,
The holy things that protect him.
He's making the serpent prow of his boat.
Meet him well,
If it is possible,
You will cross the waters that you fear;
If it is not possible,
You must come back.
I would be fool enough
To take you in!
(She leaves. Gilgamesh cries out in rage and goes off.)

Scene 16

GILGAMESH
(Still angry.)
These rocks are in my way!
(He raises axe and smashes them.)

URSHUNABI
(Entering)
What do you call yourself?
I am Urshunabi
Ferryman to Utnapishtim, the Faraway.

GILGAMESH
I am called Gilgamesh. I am from Uruk.

URSHUNABI
Why are your cheeks so starved,
Your face so drawn, such despair in your heart?
Why is your face burned in with heat and cold?
What do you search for in the world's wildernesses?

GILGAMESH
Why should I not despair?
My friend who fought at my side
Against Humbaba and the Bull of Heaven,
My friend whom I loved and with whom I endured dangers,
The end of life has overtaken him.
I wept for him seven days and nights
Until the worm entered him.
Because of my friend I fear death,
I search through the world's wildernesses.
How can I keep silent? How can I stop?
He is turned to dust and I too will be laid in dirt.
I am afraid of death,
Therefore Urshunabi,
Tell me the way to Utnapishtim.

If it is possible I will cross the waters of death,
If not, I will search the world's wildernesses.

URSHUNABI

Gilgamesh, your own hands
Have destroyed your chance to cross the waters,
When you destroyed the sacred stones,
You destroyed the safety of my boat.

GILGAMESH

Why so angry, Urshunabi?
You cross the waters by day or night,
In every season.

URSHUNABI

Those sacred stones brought me safely back.
But now go to the forest, Gilgamesh,
Cut down one hundred and twenty poles
Each sixty cubits long,
And bring them to me.
(Gilgamesh leaves.)

Scene 17

(Gilgamesh, Urshunabi.)

URSHUNABI

We've paddled for three days,
A journey of a month for ordinary craft,
And we have arrived at the waters of death.
Thrust in the first pole,
Do not let the water touch your hands.

GILGAMESH

(Thrusts it in to propel the boat.)

Look! The pole has disappeared.

The waters have eaten it!

URSHUNABI
Take the second pole, Gilgamesh.

GILGAMESH
The waters have also eaten the second pole.

URSHUNABI
Take the one hundred and twentieth pole.

GILGAMESH
The waters have eaten the one hundred and twentieth pole!
But I shall not let this defeat me.
(He holds up his arms for a mast, his shirt for a sail.)
We go to Utnapishtim, who lives east of the mountain,
To him alone of men have the gods given everlasting life.

Scene 18

UTNAPISHTIM
Who is this man walking up the beach
Behind Urshunabi, wearing lionskins?
He is no man of mine.
(Enter Gilgamesh.)
What do you call yourself,
You who have arrived here
Wearing animal skins,
With your cheeks starved and your face drawn?
Where are you hurrying to?
Why have you crossed the difficult sea?

GILGAMESH
I am Gilgamesh from the City of Uruk.

UTNAPISHTIM
If you are Gilgamesh,
Why does despair fill your heart,
Why is your face burned with heat and cold,
Why do you come here,
Searching the world's wilderness?

GILGAMESH
Why shouldn't my cheeks be starved
My face drawn,
My heart full of despair,
My face burned with heat and cold of a long journey,
Why shouldn't I search the world's wildernesses?
My friend who helped me kill the Bull of Heaven
  and Humbaba of the cedar forest,
My friend whom I loved,
With whom I shared danger,
The end of life has overtaken him.
I mourned him for seven days and nights
Until the worm entered into him.
How can I keep silent, how can I stop?
He is dust and I shall also die and be laid in the dirt.
To see Utnapishtim, whom we call the Faraway,
I have made this journey,
I have wandered the world,
Crossed the mountain ranges,
Crossed the seas and deserts,
Worn myself out with travelling,
My joints ache,
I have lost my sweet sleep.
My clothes wore out
  before I reached Siduri, the wine maker.
I killed bear, hyena, lion, panther, tiger,
Stag, ibex, and even the rabbit and gopher.
I ate their meat and wore their skins,
And that's how I reached the gate of Siduri,
Who wanted to lock me out,
Thinking me some wild criminal.

But she told me the direction;
So I found Urshunabi the ferryman
And crossed the waters of death with him.
O Utnapishtim, teacher whom I've sought
Throughout the world's wildernesses,
I wish to question you about life and death,
How shall I find the everlasting life
For which I search?

UTNAPISHTIM
There is no permanence.
Do we build a house to last forever,
Sign a contract for eternity?
What one acquires today,
He leaves to another tomorrow.
The river floods and then subsides.
The butterfly breaking its cocoon
Lives in the glory of the sun for but a day.
The sleeping and the dead are much alike.
What happens to the status of master and servant
When their doom has been fulfilled?
The judges and the mothers of destiny
decree the fate of men.
Life and death they portion out
Only the day of death they don't reveal.

GILGAMESH
All that's true, Utnapishtim,
But I look at you,
And see you are a man just like me.
I thought you'd look like a hero,
But you lie here,
Taking it easy on your back.
Tell me the truth,
How did you come to enter the company of the gods,
And to gain everlasting life?

UTNAPISHTIM

I will reveal a mystery to you,
I will tell you the secret
That no one knows except the gods and me.
You know the City Shurrupak,
Standing on the banks of the Euphrates?
In those days the world teemed,
The people multiplied,
The world bellowed like a wild bull,
And the demiurge awoke in the clamor.
Enlil said,
"The uproar of men is intolerable,
We cannot sleep there is so much noise."
They prepared to unloose the deluge
But Ea warned me in a dream,
"O man of Shurrupak,
Tear down your reed-house,
And build a reed-boat,
Abandon your possessions, seek for life,
Despise your goods and save your living soul.
Tear down your reed house, I tell you,
And build a reed-boat.
Take into the boat
The seed of all living creatures."
After I understood, I said to Ea,
What you have commanded, I will honor and do,
But what shall I tell my neighbors?
"Tell them: I have learned
Enlil is wrathful against me,
I no longer dare to live here,
I shall leave to live on the Gulf with Ea
But on you he shall rain down abundance,
Fish, wildfowl and wheat."
I built seven decks
Divided them into nine sections
With bulkheads between.
I laid in supplies.

We drank raw wine, red and white wine, oil,
We feasted while we worked
Just like it was a New Year's festival.
I myself annointed my head.
On the seventh day we finished the boat.
I loaded the boat with gold, family, kin,
Wild beasts and tame, craftsmen.
Just as Ea had foretold,
That evening the destroying rain began.
I too climbed aboard and battened down.
The god of storm turned daylight to dark,
He smashed the land like a clay pitcher.
Even the gods were terrified.
Ishtar the sweet-voiced
Cried out like a woman in labour
  "Why did I command this evil?
  Now like dead fish
  My people float in the ocean."
For six days and six nights
The storm overwhelmed the world;
On the seventh, the wind died down,
I opened the boat,
The surface of the sea stretched as flat as a roof
For as far as the eye could see.
Tears ran down my face,
For on every side all I could see was a waste of water.
Finally I saw a mountain
And there we grounded for seven days.
I let a dove loose,
But she flew back, and then a swallow,
And then a raven who, seeing the waters retreated,
Ate, flew around, cawed, and did not come back.
Then Enlil came, He swelled with anger
  "How did these mortals escape?
  Not one was to have escaped destruction!"
Ea said,
  "Enlil, how could you bring about

Such a senseless flood,
Punish the wrongdoer a little
When he breaks out,
But lash him too hard
And he perishes;
Better that a lion or wolf
Had ravaged mankind
Than the remorseless flood,
Better famine, better the plague
Had wasted mankind
Than the remorseless flood,
But I did not tell this man the secret;
The wise man learned it in a dream.
So now decide what to do with him."
Enlil took my woman and me by the hands,
He touched our foreheads to bless us,
He said,
"In time past Utnapishtim was a mortal man,
But from now he and his woman
Shall live in the distance at the mouth of rivers."
And that is how I came here.

GILGAMESH
So you have no secret formula!
My journey wasted!
You have no hidden knowledge!
Siduri was right,
What I seek I shall never find.

UTNAPISHTIM
Yes, Gilgamesh, who will bring the gods together for you,
So you can find that life you seek?
But if you wish, test yourself.
Just prevail against sleep,
For six days and seven nights.
(Gilgamesh drowses off. Utnapishtim's woman enters.)
Look at him the strong man

Who covets everlasting life,
Already the mists of sleep cover him.

WOMAN

Touch him, wake him up,
So he can return to his country in peace,
Going back the way he came.

UTNAPISHTIM

All men deny that they went to sleep.
He will try to deny it.
Therefore, bake bread, one loaf a day,
Put it by his head;
And mark the wall
To number the days he sleeps.
(They leave.)

Scene 19

(Utnapishtim, woman standing over Gilgamesh. She is putting down the seventh loaf of bread by his side.)

WOMAN

The first is dried out, the second like leather,
The third soggy, the fourth's got white specks on it,
The fifth's mouldy
And even the sixth's getting stale.

GILGAMESH

Ah-hey! Look at that!
The moment I take a catnap
You joggle my elbow to wake me up.

UTNAPISHTIM
Look. *(Points to the bread.)*

GILGAMESH
I couldn't have – I did.

UTNAPISHTIM
Wash, clean yourself.
Get ready to go back.

GILGAMESH
What can I do, Utnapishtim?
Already the thief is stealing through my body,
Death inhabits my house
Where my foot steps, there I find death.

WOMAN
Utnapishtim, you can't send him away with empty hands.
He journeyed here with effort and pain, a beggar,
You must give him a gift.

UTNAPISHTIM
Gilgamesh, you wore yourself out coming here.
What shall I give you to carry back?
I shall reveal to you a secret,
A mystery.
At the bottom of the sea grows a plant,
It will prick you like the thornbush, like the rose,
It will wound your hands.
But if any man takes it,
By tasting it, he can regain his youth!
(Gilgamesh embraces Utnapishtim who returns it. Then holds his hands above his head to indicate that all has been said.)

Scene 20

(Gilgamesh, Urshunabi.)

GILGAMESH
(Holding plant.)
Come here, look see the famous plant
Called Old Man-grows-young-again!
Whoever tastes it, is born again!
He regains his strength!
I tied stones to my feet,
Dived to the bottom of the sea,
Found it, plucked it, and brought it up.
I shall take it back to Uruk
And give it to all the old men to eat.
Now let us go bathe in that pool of water over there.

(They go to bathe, leaving the plant behind. From the pool creeps a serpent who crawls to the plant, takes it, immediately sloughs its old skin and returns to the pool. Gilgamesh and Urshunabi return laughing. Then Gilgamesh sees the plant is gone.)

GILGAMESH
Urshunabi, Urshunabi,
Was it for this I laboured with my hands,
Wrung out my heart's blood?
For myself, what have I really gained?
The beast of the earth now enjoys it.
I found and I lost!

Scene 21

(Gilgamesh, Urshunabi.)

GILGAMESH

There it is, the City of Uruk.
Urshunabi, climb up on that wall,
The outer all shining with the brilliance of burnished copper,
The seven wise men laid the foundations.
One third of the City is buildings, cunningly executed,
One third of the City is garden with rose and bird,
One third of the City is field with the temple of Ishtar within,
Goddess of love and struggle.

Scene 22

(Gilgamesh directs, Urshunabi scripts, people enact the Epic of Gilgamesh.)

CHANT OF THE PEOPLE

This too worked Gilgamesh,
The leader who knew the countries of the world,
Wise, he saw mysteries
Had knowledge of secret things,
Brought to us the account of days before the Flood;
He set out on a long journey,
Returned weary, worn out with labour,
But with the energy of renewed youth,
Engraved on a stone the entire story.

ACTORS NOTE: In the 1982 Theater of All Possibilities production, the inscriptions on Urshunabi's sacred stones (Scene 16) read:

Ideology is Hope
Belief is Love
Ritual is Faith
Society is Conscience

MAROUF THE COBBLER

Adapted to dramatic form from Sir Richard Burton's translation of the *Thousand and One Nights.*

CHARACTERS

MAROUF
FATIMAH
COOK
NEIGHBORS
RUNNER
KAZI
THE CHANGED ONE
MERCHANTS
ALI
SLAVE GIRL
BEGGARS
AN OLD WOMAN
KING
VIZIR
DUNYA
SHEIKH AL-ISLAM
PERFORMERS
PEASANT
FATHER OF HAPPINESS
SLAVE
SLAVE GIRL
BOY

Scene 1

MAROUF
(Working on repairing an old shoe, sings:)
How many nights I've spent with my wife
Sad sad misery and strife
Would to Allah when first I went in to her
With a cup of poison I'd taken her life!

FATIMAH
(Entering)
O Marouf –
I want you to bring me a vermicelli cake
All dressed with bees' honey tonight.

MAROUF
And Allah Almighty aid me to its price,
I'll bring it to you.
By Allah, I haven't got a dirham today,
But He will make it all happen.

FATIMAH
I don't know anything about all these words –
Whether He aid you or not,
Don't come home without vermicelli and bees' honey,
And if you do come without it,
I'll make your night black as your luck
When you married me and fell into my hands.
(Exits)

MAROUF
Allah is bountiful! *(Falls to his knees.)*
I beseech thee, O Lord, to grant me
The price of the kunafah
And to protect me tonight from
This wicked woman's mischief!

Scene 2

(Kunafah seller's shop. Marouf looking tearfully at the pastry cook.)

COOK

Marouf, what are you crying about?
Tell me what's happened.

MAROUF

My wife is a shrew, a raving maniac
Who tells me to bring her a kunafah;
But I have sat in my shop till past noon
And haven't even made the price
Of a loaf of plain bread.
Therefore I'm scared to death.

COOK
(Laughing)

No harm shall come to you.
How many pounds do you want?

MAROUF

Five pounds.

COOK

I have ghee, but no bees' honey;
But here's some drip honey –
That's better than bees' honey anyway.
What does it matter,
Drip honey or bees' honey?

MAROUF
(Afraid to object because he's getting credit.)

Allright. Make it drip honey.

COOK

Here now. A kunafah fit for a king.
How about some bread and cheese, too.

MAROUF

Yes.

COOK

Now, Marouf, you owe me
Four half dirhams for the bread, one for the cheese,
And five for the kunafah.
Now go to your wife, have a party,
Take this dirham for the Hammam to clean up,
And you shall have credit
For a day or two or three
Till Allah provide you with your daily bread.
And don't let your wife do without,
I will have patience with you
Till you shall have dirhams to spare.

MAROUF

(Taking up the food.)

Praised be your perfection, O Allah!
How bountiful you are!

Scene 3

(Fatimah waiting for Marouf who enters.)

FATIMAH

Did you bring the vermicelli cake?

MAROUF

Yes! Here it is.

FATIMAH

Didn't I tell you to bring it with bees' honey?
Why did you go against what I told you
And dress it with cane honey?

MAROUF

I had to buy it on credit.

FATIMAH

Loafer! Big talker!
I won't eat kunafah without bees' honey!
(Throws it at him.)
Get out, you pimp,
And bring me something else!
(She knocks out one of his teeth. He smacks her back.)
Help, O Muslims!

(Neighbors run in and free Marouf from her grip.)

FIRST NEIGHBOR

We are all happy
To eat kunafah with cane honey.
Why do you push the poor man around?
Truly, this is disgraceful.

FATIMAH

You really think so?

SECOND NEIGHBOR

Yes! He's trying very hard.

FATIMAH

Allright.

FIRST NEIGHBOR

This is so much better, Fatimah,
A little peace in the house.

FATIMAH

Yes, indeed. *(Neighbors leave.)*
I want to tell you, you imitation of a man,
That I'll never take a bite
Of this imitation of a kunafah.

MAROUF

You swear you won't eat it,
So I will eat it. *(Falls to.)*

FATIMAH

Inshallah, may the eating of it
Fill you with poison to destroy your body!

MAROUF
(Eating and laughing.)

That won't come by your bidding.
You swore you would not eat this,
But Allah is bountiful,
And He decree it,
Tomorrow night I will bring you real kunafah,
Dressed with bees honey,
And you shall eat it alone.

FATIMAH
(Baring her forearm to beat him.)

Good-for-nothing! Double-crosser! Wretch!

MAROUF
(Fleeing out.)

Give me a little time!
I'll bring you vermicelli cake!

Scene 4

(Marouf in shop with old shoe he's trying to repair. Enter runner from the Court.)

RUNNER

Up with you! The Kazi wants you at court.
Your wife has complained about you.

MAROUF

May Allah torment her!

Scene 5

(Kazi with Fatimah at his side, her arm bound-up, face smeared with blood.)

KAZI

Ho, man, have you no fear of Allah, the Most High?
Why have you beaten this good woman,
Knocked out her tooth, bloodied her face?

MAROUF

If I beat her or smashed out her tooth,
Sentence me to what you wish,
But in truth the case is
That she wanted vermicelli cake with bees' honey,
I couldn't afford it,
And the cook, my friend,
Gave me cake with cane honey on credit,
And she raised hell about it,
And is determined to do me in,
Because I can't buy her enough.
Ask the neighbors.

KAZI

O man, take this quarter dinar
And buy her some kunafah with bees' honey,
And do you and she make peace.

MAROUF

Give it to her. *(Fatimah takes money.)*

KAZI

Woman, listen to your man.
Man, deal kindly with your woman.
(They leave.)

Scene 6

(Marouf in his shop, trying to repair an old shoe.)

RUNNER
(Entering)

You are now wanted by the Kazi in the High Court.

FATIMAH
(Entering)

You thought you were going to get by without paying,
Didn't you?

MAROUF

Didn't we make peace, good woman?

FATIMAH

There endures no peace between you and me!

MAROUF

Try and catch me! I'm running away!
(Flees out.)

Scene 7

(Marouf wet, weary, enters a deserted mosque to pray, far out in the desert.)

MAROUF
Winter, wet, forced into the wilderness.
Where shall I flee this whore?
I beg you, O Allah,
To grant me someone who will take me
To a far country,
Where she won't know the way to get to me!

THE CHANGED ONE
(Entering)
O man, what ails you
That you disturb me tonight?
I have lived here for two hundred years
And have never seen anyone enter this place
And do as you do.
Tell me what you wish,
And I will accomplish your need,
Since pity for you has seized my heart.

MAROUF
Who and what are you?

THE CHANGED ONE
I am the Haunter of this Place.

MAROUF
Can you take me to a country
Where my wife, who has entoiled me
With the laws and prisons,
Because I cannot buy her all she wants,
But am reduced to endless useless work,
Where my wife will know no way to get to me?

THE CHANGED ONE
Yes. Get on my back. *(They fly.)*
We have now landed on the top of a high mountain
Overlooking the borders of China.
Mortal, descend this mountain.
You will see the gate of a city.
Enter that city, for therein
Your wife cannot come at you. *(Leaves.)*

MAROUF
I will be up with me,
And go down into that City;
Surely, there is no profit
In staying in this high land.

Scene 8

(Marouf enters the city. A small group of people: two merchants, slave girl, Ali.)

FIRST MERCHANT
O man, are you a stranger?

MAROUF
Yes.

FIRST MERCHANT
From what country?

MAROUF
From Cairo, the Auspicious.

FIRST MERCHANT
When did you leave Cairo?

MAROUF
Yesterday, at the hour of afternoon prayer.

FIRST MERCHANT
Come, O people, look at this man,
Hear what he says!

GIRL
What?

FIRST MERCHANT
He pretends he comes from Cairo
And left it at the hour of afternoon prayer!

SECOND MERCHANT
O man, how can you talk that way,
When the truth is that
A full year's journey
Lies between our City and Cairo.

MAROUF
Nobody's mad but you!
Look, here's bread I brought with me from Cairo.
And you can see, it's new.

FIRST MERCHANT
This is Cairo bread: look at it.
(Girl and second merchant laugh.)

ALI
O people, aren't you ashamed
To forget the sacred laws of hospitality,
And mock and scoff at a stranger?
Go on, be off with you and your unkind usage!
(They leave.)
Come, my brother,
No harm shall come to you from these people.
Truly, they have no shame.

Here, take my cloak.
No, O my brother, what is your name?

MAROUF

My name is Marouf,
A cobbler by trade.
I patch old shoes.

ALI

Now tell me why you left Cairo
To come to this City.

MAROUF

My wife, my friend,
Whom the people had nicknamed 'The Dung',
Was a whorish whining wretch,
Who abused and cursed me a thousand times a day,
And at last was going to send me to prison
Because I had run out of money to satisfy her wants.
I fled from her towards the Gate of Victory
And went out from the City.
There, weeping in a cell of a ruined mosque,
The Haunter of the Place came out,
Questioned me on my case, I answered,
He put me on his back,
Flew with me all night between Heaven and Earth,
Set me on yonder mountain,
And gave me to know about this City.

ALI

I myself wandered from land to land
And City to City
Until I arrived at this City, Ikhtiyan al-Khatan.
Its people, unlike those in other places,
Are hospitable flock, kindly,
And they believe you are what you say you are.
So I said to them:
I am a merchant who has preceded his packs,

And I need a place to put my baggage.
Believing me, they assigned me a lodging.
Then I said, is there any of you
Who will loan me a thousand dinars
Until my goods arrive and I repay you?
Because I need certain things before my goods come.
They gave me what I asked,
I went into the merchants bazaar,
Where I bought goods,
And sold them at fifty dinars profit the next day.
Then I consorted with the people,
Treated them liberally,
So that they loved me,
And I continued to buy and sell
Until I grew rich.
Know, O my brother,
That the proverb says,
The world is show and trickery,
And the land where nobody knows you,
There do what likes you.
So tell people you're a poor cobbler
Running away from your wife
And you'll make yourself a permanent laughing stock;
Or tell them an Ifrit brought you here,
They'll be scared to death of you and you'll be isolated.

MAROUF
What, then, shall I do?

ALI
I will tell you how to do, Inshallah!
I will give you a thousand dinars, a mule and a slave,
And you will visit some merchants
Who are my friends.
I will rise, salaam, kiss your hand, make you a great man.
I will praise your wealth and generosity;
They will believe this and love you.
So you may sell and buy and take and give with them,

And before long you'll be a man of money!
Forget your wife and live!

MAROUF
May Allah reward you!

Scene 9

(A gathering of merchants. Marouf enters with his slave.)

ALI
A blessed day, O Merchant Marouf,
O man of good works and generosity!
(Kisses his hand.)
Brothers, you are honored
By knowing the Merchant Marouf.

FIRST MERCHANT
What kind of a merchant?

ALI
Indeed, the chiefest of merchants,
There lives no wealthier than he;
His wealth and the riches of his father and forefathers
Are famous among the merchants of Cairo.
He has partners in Hind and Sind and Al-Yemen,
And is high in reputation of generosity.
Know his rank, exalt his degree,
Do him service, and know also
That he comes to this City not for trade,
But only to divert himself by seeing other people's countries.
Indeed he has no need of strangerhood
For the sake of gain and profit,
Having wealth that fires cannot consume,
And I am his servant.

SECOND MERCHANT
We are overjoyed by your visit.

FIRST MERCHANT
We hope your stay will prove profitable for you.
Consider our homes at your disposal,
Our shops open for your use.

ALI
Perhaps you have brought somewhat of silk?

MAROUF
Plenty.

FIRST MERCHANT
And yellow broadcloth?

MAROUF
Plenty.

SECOND MERCHANT
And rubies blood-red?

MAROUF
Plenty.

ALI
And long-fibered cotton?

MAROUF
Plenty.

FIRST MERCHANT
O Merchant Ali, if your countryman
Had a mind to transport a thousand costly shiffs
He could do so.

ALI
He would take them from a single one of his storehouses,
And not miss a thing.

BEGGAR
(Entering)
For the love of Allah, the Compassionate, the Merciful.
(Ali and first merchant give him a copper, the second merchant gives nothing. Marouf gives him a handful of gold.)
Allah bless you! *(Leaves)*

FIRST MERCHANT
(To second merchant and Ali:)
Truly, he gives like a king;
He gave the beggar gold without counting it.
If he weren't a man of vast wealth,
Of money without end,
He wouldn't have given the beggar a handful of gold.

POOR WOMAN
(Entering)
In the name of Allah, the Beneficient!
(Marouf also gives her a handful of gold.)
Allah bless you!

SECOND MERCHANT
In the name of Allah!

(Enter beggars. Marouf gives away all his gold – they leave calling upon Allah to bless him.)

MAROUF
(Striking hands together.)
Allah is our sufficient aid
And excellent is His agent!

FIRST MERCHANT
What bothers you, O Merchant Marouf?

MAROUF
Why, it seems that most of the people here
Are poor and needy;
If I had known of their misery
I would have loaded my saddlebags with money,
So I could have given help to the poor.
It is not in my nature to balk a beggar,
And I have no gold left,
So if a poor man came to me,
What shall I say to him?

FIRST MERCHANT
Say, Allah will send you your daily bread!

MAROUF
That's not my practice,
And that's not what's making me upset.
I wish I had another thousand dinars
To give alms with until my caravan arrives!

SECOND MERCHANT
Don't worry. Here are a thousand dinars.
Now let us go to prayers at the mosque.
(They go out to the mosque. Marouf scatters gold pieces on the heads of the worshippers. The people bless him.)

MAROUF
I need another thousand dinars!

FIRST MERCHANT
Here, give me the honor!

MAROUF
Wait till my caravan arrives,

Then if you want gold back you shall have gold,
Or if you wish precious stuffs,
You shall have them,
For there is no end to my possessions!
(Scattering gold upon the people.)

PEOPLE
May Marouf be blessed of Allah!

Scene 10

(Meeting of merchants and Ali.)

FIRST MERCHANT
He has borrowed money of everyone
In the bazaar and given it to the poor.

SECOND MERCHANT
He must owe more than sixty thousand dinars.

FIRST MERCHANT
For twenty days this has gone on,
And still no caravan!

SECOND MERCHANT
Ali, how long will your friend
Take peoples' monies and give them to the poor?

ALI
Have patience.
His caravan cannot fail to come soon.

FIRST MERCHANT
We certainly hope so.

Scene 11

(Ali, Marouf.)

ALI

O Marouf, what's going on here?
Did I tell you to brown the bread or burn it?
The merchants clamour for their coin,
They tell me you owe sixty thousand dinars,
That you have borrowed and given to the poor.
How will you satisfy these people,
Seeing that you neither buy nor sell?

MAROUF

What does it matter?
What are sixty thousand dinars?
When my caravan comes
I shall pay them off in stuffs,
Or in gold and silver,
Whatever they will.

ALI

Allah is Most Great!
Have you then a caravan?

MAROUF

Plenty.

ALI

Allah and Hell reward your impudence!
Did I teach you to say this
That you should repeat it to me?

MAROUF

Off with you and your foolish prattle!
Am I a poor man?
I have endless wealth in my caravan
And as soon as it comes,

They shall have their money's worth,
Two for one.
I have no need of them.

ALI

Thankless wretch that you are,
I'll teach you to lie to me
And not be ashamed of it.

MAROUF

Work the worst your hand can do!
They must wait till my caravan come,
When they shall have their due and more. *(Leaves)*

ALI

I praised him only a few days ago,
And if I blame him now,
I make myself out a liar,
And because of those of whom it is said:
Whoever praises and then blames
Lies twice.

(Enter merchants.)

FIRST MERCHANT

O Merchant Ali,
Have you spoken to him?

ALI

O people, I am ashamed,
Though he owes me a thousand dinars,
I can't speak to him.
When you loaned him money,
You didn't consult me,
So you have no claim on me.
Dun him yourselves,
And if he doesn't pay you,
Complain of him to the King of the City, saying:

He is an imposter who has imposed on us.
And the King will deliver you of the plague of him.

Scene 12

(King, Vizir, merchants.)

SECOND MERCHANT
O King of the Age,
We are puzzled about this Merchant Marouf,
Whose generosity is excessive.
Everything he borrows,
He gives away to the poor by handfuls.
If he were a man of no substance,
His sense wouldn't allow him to lavish gold this way;
Still, his good faith should be made manifest to us
By the coming of his caravan.
But we see none of his luggage
Although he claims he has a caravan
And has preceded it.
Now over three weeks have passed,
And he owes us sixty thousand gold pieces,
All of which he has given to the poor.

FIRST MERCHANT
He is the most generous man
I've ever seen with gold.

ALI
He does give it away right and left.

KING
Thank you, O merchants. Retire now,
And I will consider this matter.
(They leave.)

Now, Vizir,
If this man were not a merchant of vast wealth,
He had not shown all this munificence.
His caravan will assuredly come,
And then these merchants will flock to him,
And he will scatter among them riches galore.
Now I have more right to this money than they;
Therefore I have a mind to make friends with him,
Profess affection for him,
So that when his caravan arrives,
What the merchants would have had, I shall get;
And I will give him my daughter to wed
And join his wealth to my wealth.

VIZIR
O King of the Age,
I think he's nothing but an imposter,
And it's the imposter who ruins the house of the greedy.

KING
O Vizir, I will test him
And soon know if he is an imposter or true man,
Whether he is a rearling of fortune or not.

VIZIR
And how will you test him?

KING
I will send for him,
Treat him with honor,
And give him a jewel that I have.
If he know it and know its price,
He is a man of worth and wealth,
But if he does not know it,
He is an imposter and upstart,
And I will do him die
By the foulest fashion of death.

Scene 13

(King, Marouf, Vizir. After Marouf has salaamed, the King salaams in return and seats Marouf by his side.)

KING

You are the Merchant Marouf?

MAROUF

Yes.

KING

The merchants declare that you owe them
Sixty thousand gold pieces.
Is that true?

MAROUF

Yes.

KING

Then why don't you give them their money?

MAROUF

Let them wait until my caravan come,
And I shall repay them double.
If they wish for gold they shall have gold
For silver, they shall have silver,
For merchandise, they shall have merchandise.
To whomever I owe a thousand
I shall repay two thousand
To reward them for having veiled my face before the poor.
I have plenty.

KING

O merchant, take this. *(Handing the jewel.)*
What kind is it and what is its value?
(Marouf breaks it between his fingers.)
Why did you break the jewel?

MAROUF
(Laughing)
O King of the Age,
This is not a jewel.
This is but a bittock of mineral worth a thousand dinars.
Why do you style it a jewel?
A jewel I call such
As is worth three score and ten thousand gold pieces,
And this is called but a piece of mineral.
I take no account of jewel so small.
How comes it then, that you, who are a king,
Style this bit of mineral a jewel?
But you are excusable,
For that this is a poor people,
And do not have in your possession
Things of price.

KING
O merchant,
Do you have jewels such as those you speak of?

MAROUF
Plenty.

KING
Will you give me real jewels?

MAROUF
When my caravan shall come,
I will give you no end of jewels,
And all that you can desire I have plenty of
And will give you without price.

KING
O Vizir,
Tell the merchants to go their ways
And have patience with him
Till his caravan arrives,

And then come to me
To receive their monies.
(Marouf leaves.)
Now pay court to Merchant Marouf
And take and give with him in talk,
Speak to him of my daughter Dunya,
That he may wed her,
So that we can gain these riches that he has.

VIZIR

O King of the Age,
I don't like the way this man acts,
I think he is an imposter and a liar,
So don't do what you speak about
Lest you lose your daughter for nothing.

KING

O traitor,
You desire no good for me,
Because you wanted to wed my daughter,
But she would have none of you,
So now you want to block her marriage,
Let her lie fallow,
So you might take her,
But hear one word from me.
You take no concern in this matter.
How can he be an imposter and liar,
Seeing that he knew the price of the jewel,
Even what I paid for it,
And broke it because it didn't please him?
He has plenty of jewels,
And when he goes in to my daughter
And sees her to be beautiful,
She will captivate his reason
And he will love her
And give her jewels and things of price,
But you, you would forbid my daughter and myself
These good things!

Scene 14

(Vizir, King.)

VIZIR

I saw him and said,
The King loves you and has a daughter,
Winsome, lovely, to whom he's minded to marry you.
What do you say to that? He said,
No harm in that,
But let him wait till my caravan arrives,
Because a daughter of a King deserves a great wedding gift.
I have wealth in plenty
And I must make her a marriage portion of five thousand
Purses of gold.
Then I will need a thousand
To distribute to the poor and needy.
Upon my wedding night,
A thousand for those walking in her bridal procession,
A thousand to provide a feast for the troops and people,
A hundred jewels to give the princess on her wedding morning,
One jewel for each of her handmaids,
Wherewithal to clothe a thousand naked paupers,
And alms too must be given.
All this can't be done till my caravan comes,
But I have plenty,
And as soon as it is here,
I shall make no account of the outlay.

KING

Since this is his wish,
How do you dare style such a man liar and imposter?

VIZIR

I do not cease to say it.

KING

By the life of my head,

If you don't stop saying it,
I will kill you!
Go back to him, bring him here,
And I will deal with him myself!

Scene 15

(King, Marouf.)

KING
You shall not put me off with all those excuses.
Take the keys to the Treasury,
Spend all you need,
Give what you will,
Clothe the poor,
Do your desire,
Don't worry about the girl and her handmaids.
When your caravan shall have come,
Do what you will with your wife
By way of generosity
And we will have patience with you
About the marriage-portion till then,
For there is no kind of difference between me and you,
None at all.
(Signals. Kettle drums, performers, Sheikh al-Islam, Ali, Vizir.)
This is the Sheikh al-Islam.
He will write out the marriage contract.
Here is the Vizir at your service!

MAROUF
Bring out the gold and silver!

VIZIR
Must I?

KING

Obey! Else you will be a traitor!
(Marouf distributes the gold as fast as the Vizir can bring it.)

ALI

Allah and Hell visit this upon your head!
Wasn't it enough for you to squander the merchants' money,
But now you squander the King's, to boot!

MAROUF

No concern of yours,
When my caravan shall come,
I'll pay the King back royally!
(Ali turns away.)
Plague! What will happen will happen
And there is no fleeing from the Foreordained.
(Princess Dunya arrives. Marouf scatters even more money. They sit and watch the performers, who finish up and leave. Marouf strikes hands together.)
There is no Majesty and no Might
Except in Allah, the Glorious, the Great!

DUNYA

Allah preserve you!
What's wrong? What troubles you?

MAROUF

How should I not be troubled,
Seeing your father has embarrassed me,
Done me a deed like burning green corn.

DUNYA

What has my father done to you? Tell me!

MAROUF

He brought me into you before my caravan arrived,
And thus I can't give each of your handmaids a jewel,

Which I wished to do for you
  and the increasing of your dignity.
I have no need to stint myself in lavishing jewels,
For I have plenty.

DUNYA

Don't bother yourself about that.
Don't trouble yourself about me,
For I will have patience with you till your caravan come,
And when the caravan comes,
We shall get the jewels and the rest.

Scene 16

(King, Vizir.)

VIZIR
(Kissing the ground before the King's feet.)

O King of the Age,
I must tell you something,
Otherwise you may blame me for leaving you unknowing.
The Treasury is being exhausted;
Marouf has put robes of honor upon everyone,
Every day he sits, receives people, showers gold on them,
This has gone on for twenty days and no caravan has appeared.
In another ten days we shall close the Treasury on emptiness.

KING

O, Vizir, truly my son-in-law's caravan is slow in arriving,
And no news has come.

VIZIR
(Laughing)

Allah be gracious to you, O King of the Age!
You have been heedless with respect to this imposter, this liar.

As your head lives, no caravan travels toward him,
No, nor plague either, to rid us of him.
No, he has only imposed on you without let-up;
So he has wasted your treasure
And married your daughter, all for nothing.
How long, therefore, will you be heedless of this liar?

KING
O Vizir, what shall we do to learn the truth of his case?

VIZIR
O King of the Age,
None may come at a man's secrets except his wife;
So send for your daughter,
That I may question her as to the truth of his estate,
So she can question him,
And acquaint us with his case.

KING
There is no harm in that;
And as my head lives,
If it be proved that he is a liar and imposter,
I will truly do him die by the foulest of deaths!
(Daughter enters.)

DUNYA
What would you, my father?

KING
Speak with the Vizir!

DUNYA
Ho, you, the Vizir, what is your wish?

VIZIR
O my lady,
You must know that your man has squandered

Your father's substance,
Married you with no marriage-portion,
And he ceases not to promise us and break his promises,
While no tidings come of his caravan;
In short we would have you inform us concerning him.

DUNYA

Indeed his words be many,
And still he comes
And promises me jewels and treasures and costly stuffs,
But I see nothing.

VIZIR

O my lady,
This night take and give with him in talk,
Whisper to him, tell me the truth,
Don't fear me in the least,
For you are my man and I will not go against you.
So tell me the truth of the matter
And I will devise you a device
Whereby your heart may be set at rest.
Play near and far from him with words,
Profess love to him, win him to confess,
And then tell us the facts of the case.

DUNYA

O my papa, I know how I will test him.

Scene 17

(Marouf, Dunya.)

DUNYA

O my beloved,
O coolth of my eyes, O fruit of my vitals,
Allah never desolate me with your loss,
Nor time sunder us two, you and me.
Indeed the love of you has homed in my heart,
The fire of passion has consumed my liver,
Nor will I ever forsake you,
Or go against you.
But I would have you tell me the truth,
For the shifts of falsehood do not profit,
Nor do they gain credit for all seasons.
How long will you impose on my father and lie to him?
I fear that your affair be discovered to him,
Before we can devise some device,
And he will lay violent hands upon you.
So acquaint me with the facts of the case,
Nothing shall happen to you except to gladden you.
When you have spoken truly,
Don't fear that harm will befall you.
How often will you declare you are a merchant, rich,
And have a caravan?
For a long time now you say my caravan, my caravan!
But no sign appears of your goods,
Your face shows your anxiety.
Now if there is no value in your words,
Tell me, and I will contrive you a contrivance
So that you come off safe, Inshallah!

MAROUF

I will tell you the truth,
Then do what you will.

DUNYA
Speak, and look you speak truly,
For truth is the ark of safety,
And beware of lying,
It dishonors the liar.

MAROUF
Know then, my lady,
That I am no merchant and have no caravan;
No, I was but a shoemaker in my own country,
And had a wife called Fatimah the Dung
Who drove me out of the City into the desert,
A Changed One took me to the top of yonder mountain,
Ali I found here, he told me to say I had plenty
Of whatever anyone asked me about, and so –

DUNYA
Truly you are clever
In the practice of lying and imposture!

MAROUF
O my lady, may Allah the Mighty preserve you
To veil sins and countervail chagrins!

DUNYA
Look, you imposed upon my father,
And deceived him by your deluding boasts,
So that out of greed for gain
He married me to you.
Then you squandered his wealth,
And the Vizir bears you a grudge for this.
Many times he spoke against you,
Calling you a liar and imposter.
But my father would not listen to him,
Because the Vizir had tried to wed me
But I would not consent to it.
However, time has stretched out, my father doubted,
And he told me, make him confess.

So I have made you to confess
And what was covered is discovered.
Now my father proposes mischief for you because of this,
But you have become my man,
And I will not go against you.
If I told my father what I've learned from you,
That you impose on kings' daughters and squander wealth,
He would slay you without a doubt.
Then it would be noised among the people
That I had married such a man, and my honor be smirched.
Furthermore, if he kill you,
Probably he would require me to marry that other,
And I will never consent to such a thing,
No, not though I die!
So rise, dress in a Mameluke's dress,
Take these fifty thousand dinars of my money,
Mount a swift steed,
And get you to land beyond the boundaries
of my father's rule.
Then make yourself a merchant,
Send me a letter by private courier,
That I may know where you live,
So that I can send you all my hand can garner.
Thus your wealth shall wax great,
And if my father die, I'll send for you,
You can return with respect and honor,
And if we die, you or I,
And go to the mercy of Allah the Most Great,
Resurrection will unite us.
This, then, is the right way:
And while we both live and are well
I will not cease to send you letters and monies.
Arise before dawn and vengeance light upon your head!

MAROUF
O my lady,
Say farewell with your embrace.

DUNYA
No harm in that.

Scene 18

(King, Vizir, Dunya.)

KING
O my daughter, what do you have to say?

DUNYA
I say, Allah blacken your Vizir's face,
Because he would have blackened my face
In my man's eyes!

KING
How so?

DUNYA
He came into me yesterday,
But before I could begin the matter with him,
In walked Faraj, the Chief Eunuch,
A letter in his hand for Marouf, and said
Ten white slaves stand under the palace window
And they gave me this letter,
Saying they were servants of Merchant Marouf,
And brought him news of his caravan.
I took and read the letter as follows:
From the five hundred Mamelukes
To our Master, Merchant Marouf:
After you left us,
The Bedouins came out and attacked us.
They were two thousand horse to our five hundred
And the running battle with them took thirty days,
This is why we are late.
They succeeded in taking two hundred bales of cloth

And killed fifty of us –
When I gave the letter to my man, he cried,
Allah disappoint them!
What possessed them to fight the Bedouin
Over two hundred bales of merchandise?
What are two hundred bales? Only seven thousand dinars.
I shall go out and hasten them.
I will count what the Bedouins took as charity.
Then he left me, laughing,
Showing no concern over the wastage of his wealth,
Or the slaughter of his slaves.
As soon as he left, I looked through the lattice
And saw the ten Mameluke,
Each clad in clothes that we do not have the equal of here.
He left with them to bring up his caravan,
And hallowed be Allah who hindered me
From saying anything you told me to,
For he would have mocked you and me,
And perhaps even have given me the eye of disparagement
And hated me.
But the fault is all your Vizir's
Who speaks badly against my man.

KING
O my daughter, your man's wealth is indeed endless,
And he does not count it,
For he has done nothing since coming to our City
But give out bounty to the poor.
Inshallah, he will speedily return with the caravan,
And good in plenty will flow to us from him.
Now, Vizir, if you do not cease being a traitor,
It shall be you who suffer for it.

Scene 19

(Marouf, peasant.)

MAROUF
Indeed the ways are walled up before my face,
Death is as good or better than jeering life.
(Sees peasant.)
Peace be with you!

PEASANT
Welcome, my Lord.
Are you one of the Sultan's Mamelukes?

MAROUF
Yes.

PEASANT
Stop with me for a while and eat.

MAROUF
O my brother, you are of the liberal,
But I see nothing with you for you to feed me with,
How then, do you invite me?

PEASANT
The town is near. I will go fetch dinner for you.

MAROUF
I can go there as quickly as you can,
Buy what I have a mind to in the bazaar, and eat.

PEASANT
O my Lord, it is but a little village,
And there's no bazaar either for buying or selling,
So I conjure you by Allah,
Stay here and hearten my heart,
I will run there and be back quickly. *(Leaves)*

MAROUF

I have taken this poor man from his work;
So I will plough in his place until he gets back,
To make up for having hindered him.
(Plough strikes ring of gold. He finds a casket of jewels and gold. Inside is a ring that he rubs.)

FATHER OF HAPPINESS
(Voice:)

Adsum! Here am I, at your service, my Master.
Ask and it shall be given you.
Will you build a City, destroy a capital,
Kill a king, dig a river-channel,
Whatever you seek, it shall come to pass,
By the leave of King of All-Might,
Creator of day and night.

MAROUF

O creature of Allah,
Who and what are you?

FATHER OF HAPPINESS
(Appearing)

I am the slave of this seal ring,
Bound to the service of him who possesses it.
Whatever he seeks, I accomplish for him,
I have no excuse in neglecting whatever he bids me to do,
Because I am Sultan over two-and-seventy tribes of Jinns,
Each one of which thousand rules a thousand Marids,
Each Marid a thousand Ifrits,
Each Ifrit a thousand Satans,
Each Satan over a thousand Jinns:
And they are all under my command,
And may not gainsay me.
As for me, I am spelled to this seal ring,
You have gotten hold of it,
And I become your slave;
So ask what you will,

For I hear your word and obey your bidding,
And if you have need of me at any time,
By land or by sea,
Rub the ring and you will find me with you.
But do not rub it twice in succession,
Or you will consume me with the fire
Of the names graven on it,
And thus lose me and regret me.
Now I have acquainted you with my case and – Behold!

MAROUF
What is your name?

FATHER OF HAPPINESS
My name is Abu al Sa'adat, Father of Happiness.

MAROUF
O Abu al Sa'adat, what is this place,
Who enchanted you in this casket?

FATHER OF HAPPINESS
O my Master, this casket is but the beginning
Of the treasure called the Hoard of Shaddad, son of Ad,
He who laid the foundation of many-columned Iram,
The like of which has never been seen among the lands.
I was his slave in his life-time,
And this his seal ring,
Which he laid up in his treasure,
And which fell to your lot.

MAROUF
Can you transport this Hoard anywhere upon the earth?

FATHER OF HAPPINESS
Yes! Nothing easier.

MAROUF
Can you bring me he-mules

And chests and fill the chests with treasures?
And load them upon the mules?

FATHER OF HAPPINESS
Nothing easier!

MAROUF
O Abu al-Sa'adat,
Can you bring me loads of some costly stuffs?

FATHER OF HAPPINESS
Would you have Egyptian stuffs,
Or Syrian or Persian or Indian or Greek?

MAROUF
Bring me a hundred loads of each,
On five hundred mules.

FATHER OF HAPPINESS
O Master, give me delay
So that I may dispose my Marids,
And send a company to each country,
To fetch a hundred loads of its stuffs,
And then take the form of he-mules to return with the stuffs.

MAROUF
How much time do you want?

FATHER OF HAPPINESS
The time of the blackness of night.
Day shall not dawn
Before you have all that you desire.

MAROUF
I grant you the time. Be gone.

FATHER OF HAPPINESS
First, this slave of mine shall set you a feast.

(Enter slave with feast set of silver. Father of Happiness leaves. Enter peasant with lentils and barley bag.)

PEASANT
Would I'd killed a couple of chickens
And fired them red in ghee to give the Sultan!

MAROUF
(To the slave:)
Bring him here!
(Brings peasant before Marouf.)
What is this?

PEASANT
Your dinner. Excuse me,
I had not thought the Sultan had come,
Otherwise I would have killed a couple of chickens
And served you in goodly style.

MAROUF
The Sultan hasn't come.
I'm his son-in-law and was angry at him.
But he's sent his officers to make peace with me,
And now I'm minded to go back to the City.
But you made me this guest meal without knowing me,
And I accept it from you, lentils though it be,
And won't eat except of your cheer,
Also let me give you this pot of gold,
Then come to me in the City
And I will treat you with honor.

Scene 20

(King, Vizir)

KING

O Vizir, indeed my heart is concerned
For my son-in-law; for I fear the Bedouins may kill him.
I would to Heaven I knew where he was bound
So I could follow with my troops!

VIZIR

Allah be merciful to you for your heedlessness!
As your head lives, the rascal saw
That we were awake to him, feared dishonor, and fled,
For he is nothing but an imposter, a liar.

FATHER OF HAPPINESS
(Entering)

O King of the Age,
Allah grant you permanent glory, prosperity, and long life!

KING

Who are you and what is your business?

FATHER OF HAPPINESS

I am a courier, and your son-in-law
Who is come with his caravan
Sends me to you with a letter and here it is!
After salutations galore to our uncle the glorious King!
Know that I am at hand with the caravan,
So come forth to meet me with the troops.

KING

Allah blacken your brow, O Vizir!
How often will you blacken my son-in-law's name,
Calling him liar and imposter?
See, he's come with his caravan
And you're nothing but a traitor.

VIZIR

O King of the Age,
I said it only because of the long delay of the caravan,
And because I feared the loss of your wealth
That he wasted.

KING

O traitor! What are my riches?
Now that his caravan has come
He will give me great plenty in their place.
(Enter Dunya)
Good news for you!
Your husband will be here soon with his caravan,
He has sent me a letter to that effect
And I'm going forth to meet him.
(King and Vizir leave.)

DUNYA

A wondrous thing!
Was he laughing at me, mocking me
Or did he have mind to test me,
When he told me he was a pauper?
But Glory to Allah, I failed not in my duty to him!

Scene 21

(Ali, merchants, people.)

ALI

Why is the City all decorated?

FIRST MERCHANT

The caravan of Marouf,
The King's son-in-law, is come!
(Turns away.)

ALI

Allah is Almighty! What a calamity is this man!
He came to me, fleeing his wife, a poor man.
Where then could he get a caravan?
The King's daughter must have devised it for him,
Fearing his disgrace.
May Allah the Most High veil his success
And not bring him to public shame!
(Enter King, Vizir, Marouf, Father of Happiness.)

FIRST MERCHANT

Look over there! The King, Marouf,
The Vizir, Marouf's servant are watching
The caravan enter the City!

SECOND MERCHANT

It's so rich the gallbladder of a lion would burst with envy!

ALI

(To Marouf:)

You have played out this trick,
And it has prospered to your hand,
O Sheikh of imposters!
But you deserve it
And Allah the Most High increase your bounty!

MAROUF

(Laughing. Then to Father of Happiness:)

Carry the loads of gold into the treasury
Of my uncle the King,
Open the bales of cloth and bear the best
To Princess Dunya
That she may distribute them to her handmaids,
And take to her also the coffer of jewels
That she may choose and divide the remainder.
And give me the box of gold first
That I may repay these merchants,

Two thousand for each one thousand they loaned me,
And then give gold pieces to all the King's soldiers.

FATHER OF HAPPINESS
I hear your words, and I obey your bidding.
(Marouf hands out gold to merchants. Father of Happiness leaves with Vizir.)

KING
Enough of this giving, O my son!
There is but little left.

MAROUF
I have plenty!
(Aside) And indeed why should I count my giving
When the Slave of the seal ring brings me what I seek?

VIZIR
(Returning)
O King of the Age,
The treasury is full indeed
And will not hold the rest of the loads.
Where shall we put the rest of the golds and jewels?

KING
Use my private palace on the lake.
(Vizir leaves.)

DUNYA
(Entering)
I wish I knew how he came by all this wealth!

ALI
I wonder how he's lied and swindled
That he's got all these treasures?
If they'd come from the King's daughter,
He wouldn't waste them this way.
How excellent is his saying who said:

When Kings' King gives, reverently pause
And don't inquire into the cause:
Allah gives his gifts to whom He will,
So respect and abide by His holy laws!

DUNYA
(To Marouf:)
Did you mock me,
Or were you testing me with your story
Of being a poor man and fugitive from your wife?
Praised be Allah I failed not my duty to you!
For you are my beloved,
And there's none dearer to me than you,
Whether you be rich or poor.
But I would have you tell me
What you did design by those words.

MAROUF
I wanted to test you,
And see whether your love was sincere
Or for the sake of wealth and greed of worldly good.
But now it's manifest to me your affection is true,
And since you are a true woman, welcome to you,
I know your worth!
(Rubs his seal ring, Father of Happiness appears.)

FATHER OF HAPPINESS
Adsum at your service! Ask what you will.

MAROUF
I want a treasure-suit
And treasure-trinkets for my woman,
Including a necklace of forty unique jewels.

FATHER OF HAPPINESS
To hear is to obey.

(Slave runs in with objects.)

DUNYA
O my man, I will treasure these up
For holidays and festivals.

MAROUF
Wear them at any time
For I have others in plenty.

Scene 22

(King, Vizir.)

KING
O Vizir, consider all that's happened.
What do you say now about this affair?

VIZIR
O King of the Age, no merchant acts this way.
A merchant keeps a piece of linen with him for years,
And doesn't sell it except at a profit.
How should a merchant have generosity like this generosity,
And where should he get the like of these treasures and stuffs,
Of which only a small fraction is found with kings?
So how should loads of it be found with a merchant?
There needs must be a cause for this,
And if you will listen to me,
I will make the truth of this case manifest to you.

KING
O Vizir, I will do your bidding.

VIZIR
Here comes your son-in-law.

Tell him that you wish us to relax
Together in this flower-garden.
We will call for wine,
I will there ply him with,
Compel him to drink, to lose his reason,
And then his judgement will forsake him.
Then we will question him of the truth of his case,
And he will discover to us his secrets,
For wine is a traitor,
And Allah-gifted is he who said –
  When we drank wine and it crept its way
  To the place of Secrets, I cried, O stay!
  In fear lest its influence take my wits
  And my friends spy matters that hidden lay.
After he has told us the truth,
We shall know his case,
And then deal with him as we please.
I fear for you the consequences of his present style:
Perhaps he may covet the kingdom
And win over your troops by lavish generosity
And so depose you and take your kingdom from you.

KING
You have spoken well. *(Marouf enters.)* Marouf!
O my son-in-law, let us divert ourselves,
You, the Vizir and I.

MAROUF
No harm in that.

VIZIR
(Clapping hands. Servant appears with wine.)
Take the cup of the drink
To which Reason bows its neck in reverence.

MAROUF
What is this, O Vizir?

VIZIR

This is the longing virgin,
And the maid long kept at home,
The giver of joy to hearts,
Whereof spoke the poet:
  So subtle is her essence it would seem
  Through every limb like course of soul she runs.
And Allah-gifted is he who said:
  Wine-cup and ruby-wine high worship claim
  Dishonor 'twere to see their honor waste:
  Bury me when I'm dead by side of vine,
  Whose veins shall moisten bones in clay misplaced;
  Nor bury me in rock and wild, for I
  Dread only after death no wine to taste.

MAROUF

O, to drink and listen to your poetry,
What more is there than to suck the cup lip?

VIZIR

Well-said, better done, let us drink again!

MAROUF

Moon, stars, night, universe, life, death –

VIZIR

(With glance at King.)

By Allah, O Merchant Marouf,
I admire how you got those jewels
Whose like the King of Chosroes doesn't possess!
In all our lives we never saw a merchant
Who has heaped up riches like yours,
Or more generous than you,
For your doings are the doings of kings
And not of merchants.
Therefore, Allah's blessings upon you,
Aquaint me with all this,
That I may know your rank and condition.

MAROUF

I'm neither merchant nor king!
(Laughs)

VIZIR

Who are you, then, what is your condition?
Drink, O my brother.

MAROUF

(Drunkenly)

I'm a poor cobbler from Cairo
Who fled his whorish brutal wife,
And went out the Gate of Victory to pray upon the desert.
A Changed One flew me to the top of yonder mountain.
I entered your City, mocked for being a poor stranger,
Then, Merchant Ali loaned me a thousand dinars,
Told me to say I had plenty of whatever was asked,
And I gave everything away that was given to me,
Until I had to flee because you were too suspicious,
And then I found this ring,
That when rubbed produces the Father of Happiness
Who gives me whatever I seek.

VIZIR

I conjure you by Allah,
O my Lord Marouf, show us this ring
That we may see its make.

MAROUF

Take it and look upon it.

VIZIR

If I rub it, its slave will appear?

MAROUF

Yes. Rub it and he will appear to you.
And do you divert yourself by looking at him.
(Vizir rubs ring.)

FATHER OF HAPPINESS
(Appearing)
Adsum at your service, O my Master!
Ask and it shall be given you.
Will you ruin a City or build a capital?
Whatever you seek, I will do for you, without fail.

VIZIR
Take up that wretch,
Cast him down in the most desolate of desert lands,
Where he shall find nothing to eat or drink,
So he may die of hunger, perish miserably,
And none may know of him.
(Father of Happiness grabs Marouf.)

MAROUF
O Abu al-Sa'adat, where will you go with me?

FATHER OF HAPPINESS
I go to cast you down in the Desert Quarter,
O ill-bred scum with stupidity for a brain!
Shall one have the like of this talisman here,
And give it to the people to gaze at?
Truly you deserve what has befallen you,
And except that I fear Allah,
I would let you fall from a height of a thousand fathoms
And let the winds tear you to shreds. *(They leave.)*

VIZIR
What do you think of me now?
Didn't I tell you this fellow was a liar, an imposter,
But you wouldn't believe me?

KING
You were right, O my Vizir,
Allah grant you happiness,
But now give me the ring,
That I may solace myself with the sight.

VIZIR

O lackwits,
Why should I give it to you and stay your servant,
After I have become your master?
But I will waste you no more on life.
(Rubs ring. Father of Happiness appears.)
Take this ill-mannered churl away
And cast him down by his son-in-law and swindlerman.
(Father of Happiness grabs King.)

KING

O creature of my Creator, what is my crime?

FATHER OF HAPPINESS

I don't know but my master has commanded me,
And I can't go against whoever has the enchanted ring.
(They leave.)

Scene 23

(Vizir, merchants, Dunya, people. Father of Happiness by Vizir's side.)

VIZIR

O people,
I have done away with Marouf and your King,
I have had the Slave of this seal ring
To cast them down into the Desert Quarter,
And unless you make me Sultan over you,
I will bid the Slave of the seal ring
To take you up one and all
And to cast you down into the Desert Quarter
Where you shall die of hunger and thirst.

FIRST MERCHANT

Do us no damage,

For we accept you as Sultan over us,
And will not in any way go against your bidding.

ALL
You are our Sultan!

VIZIR
Now leave me and your Princess alone.
(They leave.)
Make yourself ready,
For I mean to come in to you tonight,
Because I long for you with love.

DUNYA
Have patience with me
Till my period of widowhood be ended,
Then draw up your contract of marriage with me,
And go in to me according to law.

VIZIR
I don't recognize any period of widowhood,
Nor have I any mood to delay;
I don't need a contract,
Nor do I know lawful from unlawful
But I need to go in to you tonight!

DUNYA
So be it, then, and welcome to you!

Scene 24

(Vizir, Dunya. Vizir enters Dunya's bedroom.)

DUNYA
A blessed night!

But if you had killed my man and father,
It had been more to my mind.

VIZIR
There is no help but I kill them.
(Dunya smiles at and caresses him. Vizir attempts to embrace her.)

DUNYA
O my Lord, don't you see the man looking at us?
I conjure you, by Allah, screen me from his eyes!
How can you know me while he looks at us?

VIZIR
(Angrily)
Where is this man?

DUNYA
There, in the bezel of the ring!
Putting out his head and staring at us!

VIZIR
(Laughing)
Don't be afraid.
He's only the Slave of the seal ring,
And he is subject to me.

DUNYA
I am afraid of Ifrits;
Pull it off and throw it far from me.

(Vizir takes it off, then approaches her, she kicks him in the stomach, knocking him backwards. She seizes ring and rubs it.)

FATHER OF HAPPINESS
Adsum at your service, O my Mistress!

DUNYA
Take up this infidel,
Clap him in prison, chain him there.
(Father of Happiness takes Vizir out, returns.)

FATHER OF HAPPINESS
I have laid him in the Prison of Wrath.

DUNYA
Fetch my man and father at once!
(Father of Happiness leaves, and enter Marouf and King.)
O my papa, sit upon your throne,
Be King as before,
And make my man your Vizir,
And tell your troops what has happened.
Then send for your Vizir in prison,
Do him die, and afterward burn him
For he is a miscreant
And would have gone in to me with lewdness,
And has testified against himself
That he is an infidel and believes in no religion.
And do tenderly by your son-in-law.

KING
Hearing and obeying, O my daughter.
But give me the ring or give it to your man.

DUNYA
I will keep the ring myself,
And it's very likely I will be more careful of it than you.
Whatever you wish, seek it of me
And I will demand it for you of the Slave of the seal ring.
So don't fear any harm as long as I live,
And after my death do what you two will with the ring.

Scene 25

(Dunya, Marouf.)

DUNYA

O Marouf, we have had happy years together,
When my father died six years after our marriage,
I made you Sultan,
And our little boy is now five years old,
But I am ill and like to die.

MAROUF

Allah preserve you, O darling of my heart!

DUNYA

No, my time is come,
But you must take equal care of this ring and the boy.

MAROUF

No harm shall come to him who Allah protects!

DUNYA

Here is the ring. Now you must govern alone.

Scene 26

(Marouf retiring for the night, a slavegirl kneading his feet, he falls to sleep. Fatimah creeps in and lies beside him.)

MAROUF
(Awakening)

I seek refuge with Allah from Satan the stoned!
Who are you, you ugly woman?

FATIMAH

Don't be afraid,

I am your wife, Fatimah al-Urrah.

MAROUF

How did you get here? Who brought you here?
When did you leave Cairo?

FATIMAH

Know that when you and I fell out,
And Iblis prompted me to do you damage,
I complained of you to the kazis,
And the judges tried to lay hold of you
But couldn't find you.
Then after two days past,
Repentance got hold upon me,
And I knew the fault was with me,
But weeping availed me nothing,
My money ran out, I was obliged to beg my bread.
So I fell to begging of everyone,
From the courted rich to the condemned poor,
And since you left
I've eaten fully of the bitterness of beggary,
Every night I bewept our separation
And all that I had suffered from your leaving,
Humiliation and ignominy, abjection and misery.
But yesterday, I went about begging all day,
No one gave me anything;
As often as I accosted anyone and craved a crust,
He cursed me and gave me nothing.
I went to bed supperless, hunger burned me,
A sore on me was that which I suffered,
And behold one appeared, and said
Woman, why are you weeping?
I said, I used to have a husband
Who provided for me and fulfilled my wishes,
But now he's lost to me, I don't know where he is,
And I have been in desperate straits since he left me.
He said, what is your husband's name?
I answered, Marouf.

I know him, he said. He is now Sultan of a certain City,
And if you will, I will carry you to him.
Cried I, I am under your protection,
By your bounty bring me to him!
He took me, flew with me between Heaven and Earth,
And said, enter that chamber and find your husband asleep.
Indeed I had not thought you would forsake me,
Who are your mate,
Praised be Allah who has united you with me!

MAROUF

Did I forsake you or you forsake me?
You complained of me to the judges
And finally to the High Judge
Who sent police after me,
So that I had to flee my own City.

FATIMAH

That which happened was foreordained of Allah,
But I repent me and I place myself under your protection,
Beseeching you not to abandon me,
And let me eat bread with you by way of alms.

MAROUF

Repent from mischief and stay with me,
And nothing shall happen to you but what pleasures you,
But if you work any wickedness
I will kill you, fearing no one.
Don't think you can complain of me to the High Court here,
Because I am become Sultan and the people dread me,
But I fear no one save Allah Almighty,
Because I have a talismanic ring,
And when I rub it, its Slave appears to me.
So what do you wish, I will cause it to be provided:
To return to your own country with abundance for your life,
Or to stay here with me where I will provide you
With a palace and furnish it with silk and handmaidens,
Dainty dishes and sumptuous suits,

And you shall be a Queen and live in all delight
Until you die or I die. What do you say?

FATIMAH
I wish to stay with you.

Scene 27

(Boy, slave girl.)

BOY
I tried to visit Fatimah as I do my father,
But she hates me because I'm not her son,
And so now I stay away and dislike her.

SLAVE GIRL
Yes, Marouf himself does not bother with her,
For she has grown to be a grizzled old fright,
A baldheaded blight, loathlier than the snake
Speckled black and white, and more
Because beyond measure she had used to treat him so evilly
As the proverb says:
Ill-usage the root of desire digs up,
And sows hate in the soil of hearts.
And Allah-gifted is he who spoke:
Beware of losing men's hearts by injurious deeds;
For when Aversion take his place none may Love restore:
Hearts when affection leaves them are like glass
Which broken, can't be made whole –
it's broke forevermore.

BOY
Marouf only gave her shelter, I think,
Not for any good quality in her,
But out of desire for approval of Allah Almighty.

Scene 28

(Boy, Fatimah. Fatimah steals across courtyard at night.)

FATIMAH

Marouf will have nothing to do with me,
And he makes love to his beautiful concubines.
I will take the seal ring from him,
Because he lays it to one side when he makes love,
Kill him, and make myself Queen.

BOY

What's into this witch,
To leave her lodging at night,
And make for my father's pavilion?
There needs to be some reason for this.
I will take my sword and follow her.
My father laughs, Mahallah,
That's a mighty fine sword, my son,
But you have not taken it to battle nor cut off a head.
But I will not fail to cut off a head
That deserves cutting.

Scene 29

(Marouf laying sleeping with slave girl. Fatimah enters, looks for the seal ring.)

FATIMAH

Here it is. *(Starts to rub it.)*

BOY
(Entering)

No! *(Strikes her down.)*

MAROUF
What is this, my son?

BOY
O my father, how often you have said to me,
You have a mighty fine sword
But you have not used it in battle nor cut off a head.
And how often I answered you saying,
I will not fail to cut off a head that deserves cutting.
And now, see, I have cut off for you
A head well worth the cutting!
She took the seal ring from you to kill you.

MAROUF
(Taking seal ring from dead woman.)
You are indeed my true son,
Without question or dispute;
Allah ease you in this world and the next
As you eased me of this vile woman!
Her attempt led only to her own destruction
And Allah-gifted is he who said:
When Allah's aid forwards a man's intent
His wish in every case shall find consent;
But if that aid of Allah be refused
His first attempt shall do him damagement.
Her coming from Cairo was but to her grave
And thanks to Allah for him who said
We tread the steps appointed for us,
And he whose steps are appointed must tread them.
He whose death is decreed to take place in our land
Shall not die in any land but that.

Scene 30

SLAVE GIRL

And after this King Marouf
Sent for the peasant whose guest he had been
When he was a fugitive
And made him Vizir and Chief Counsellor.
And learning he had a daughter of beauty and loveliness,
Of qualities nature-enobled at birth
And exacted of worth
He took her as his woman,
And in due course married off his son.
So they abode awhile in all solace of life and its delight
And their days were serene and their joys untroubled,
Till there came to them
The Destroyer of delights and the Sunderer of societies,
The Depopulator of populous places
And the Orphaner of sons and daughters.
And glory be to the Living who does not die
And in whose hands are the Keys to the Seen and Unseen!

FAUST

Part One

Translated and adapted to dramatic form from Goethe's *Faust, Part One.*

CHARACTERS

VOICE
FAUST
WAGNER
MEPHISTOPHELES
SPIRITS
FROSCH
BRANDER
SIEBEL
ALTMAYER
WITCH
SHE-APE
HE-APE
MARGARETA
MARTHA
LISBETH
VALENTINE
WILL-O-THE-WISP
WITCHES
WARLOCKS
HUCKSTER-WITCH
YOUNG WITCH
OLD WITCH

Scene 1

VOICE

The devil's never made me hate him,
Even by this last request to tempt my servant, Faust.
Man's active nature, lazy,
Grows satisfied too soon.
He learns to crave convenient comfort;
Therefore I cheerfully gave him a comrade
Who tempts him, excites him, tests him,
And so the devil creates, despite his will,
Though he's the spirit of denial.
But you, who are my sons in truth,
Enjoy the rich, the ever-living beauty!

(Night. Faust restless at a desk.)

FAUST

I've now studied Philosophy,
Law, Medicine, and even, alas! Theology
From one end to the other.
But what an idiot!
I'm no wiser than before,
I'm called Professor, yea, Doctor,
And up and down and left and right
I've led my students by the nose
For ten long years –
And now I see that nothing can be known!
This knowledge cuts me to the quick.
Of course, I'm smarter than the competition;
Those canting teachers, preachers, doctors;
My doubts and scruples I've overcome;
I'm not afraid of State or Church,
And in return have lost my joy
Knowing now that I cannot know certainty,
Knowing now I cannot help another man.
In addition, my studies have made me poor,

I own no land, no money, no title.
No dog would live my life!
Therefore, I turn to Magic;
I hope to reach the secrets
Through spirit-power and spirit-speech
And end this stupidity
Of spouting off about what I don't understand.
I want to discover the inmost force
That binds and guides the world,
Explore everything, suck it to the marrow.
And never speak an empty word again.

This dreary damned study's a prison.
No sunlight except through painted glass.
Books! stacked, toppling over,
Gray with dust, worm-eaten,
Full of silver fish,
My papers stuck in, around them,
My glasses, boxes, instruments!
Inherited junk packed and jammed!
This is my world –
If such can be called a world.

Why do I hesitate?
Why am I oppressed with unknown needs?
What holds back my life's flow?
Because instead of living Nature
Where God intended me,
I surround myself
With bones and death and rules!

(Enter Wagner.)

WAGNER

Pardon me, I heard your declamation –
Wasn't it from a Greek tragedy?
I should like to be indoctrinated with the art –

Then people would listen to my scholarship.
I've even heard it said
That priests could learn from actors.

FAUST

Yes, if the priest's an actor by nature,
Which does happen now and then.

WAGNER

But sir, when our scholarship
Ties us down without a holiday
Not only winter, but spring and summer,
How shall our counsels lead the world?

FAUST

You'll never do it without deep feeling.
You'll never get across
Unless your soul fills your art with force
To vibrate each listening heart a little faster.
But you keep on using your scissors and glue,
Scrap together a book from other men's feasts,
From your ashheap blow up a little fire;
Some apes and children will admire you
If that's what you want.
But unless you speak from your heart
No one will ever hear you.

WAGNER

Style is what speakers are judged by.
And that's what I wish to learn.

FAUST

Be honest, if you want to win.
Don't be a formal fool.
Commonsense and intelligence
Don't need a rulebook.
If your mind's concentrated on a truth,

Do you need an encyclopedia?
No, these polished speeches,
Where your thought's cut-up confetti,
They're as dreary
As winds rattling dried up leaves.

WAGNER
Ah, sir, art is long
But our life is very short
And often in the middle of my studying
My head and heart are seized with fear.
It's hard to learn everything
So that man can reach the source!
Before a man's half-way there,
More often than not a man's dropped dead.

FAUST
Are books, then, your well
Where you hope to quench your thirst?
You'll stay thirsty
Till you can drink from your own soul.

WAGNER
Forgive me! Nothing exceeds the pleasure
Of studying traces of the spirit's past,
Criticize the old ideas, totems and taboos,
And see how high we've evolved.

FAUST
Oh yes! Evolved right up to the Galaxy!
Look, my friend: the antique gods
Are now a book protected by seven seals.
What you call History
Is but the history of your professors,
Whose mirror hardly reflects a single ray.
That's why history bores everyone,
Like an old dump or sewerage pit,

Or at best a melodrama,
Stuffed full of moral cliches
Suitable to puppets.

WAGNER
But, the world! the heart! the mind!
We must try to understand them.

FAUST
What do you understand of understanding?
Who dares call that child by its real name?
The few who did understand
And talked generously to the masses
Laying bare their conscience
They were always crucified or burned.
Excuse me, Wagner, it's midnight
And our talk must end.

WAGNER
I could stay up much longer
And listen to whatever you expound.
But, sir, tomorrow I'll ask more questions.
I've learned a lot, consumed a thousand books,
But all knowledge is my ambition. *(Exits)*

FAUST
The only mind that stays optimistic
Is the kind digging greedily in junkpiles
Gloating over each shirtbutton.
And that nasally grovel
Dared interrupt my meditation!
But maybe I should thank
This boring thesis writer,
Since I, the image of God, they say,
Began by assuming Eternal Truth
To be my right for a few years' study,
Decided to be enlightened,

And not my passion's slave,
Planned to pulse in Nature's veins,
To reach beyond, create with the gods,
And found myself too late
Tied down to the image of lying bookworm.
I'm thrown back on Man's uncertain fate.
Who will teach me?
Should I do this or that?
Not understanding, whether we do or don't do,
Our life's possibilities diminish daily.
Whatever we see by spirit's intuition
Turns into the opposite from some alien mechanism.
If we achieve this world's facts,
We call values vain imagination.
Positive emotions turn negative,
Then disappear from sight.
Once we dealt with infinites
But quickly submit to dull routine.
Anxiety and guilt consume our hearts,
Work in their silent ceaseless poison,
Killing all joy and serenity,
Their images projected in turn as
House, property, wife, children,
Fire, water, storm and grave.
We dread the accidents that never come.
Perform funerals for what we never lose.

I am not like the gods –
That truth cuts too deep!
I am like a worm,
Working and living in dust
Until a stranger steps on me.
Isn't this university life a heap of dust?
Where shall I find any help here?
Here a thousand books
Teach me only that self-tortured men
Live on and on in misery.

Here and there a happy man, but lonely.
Why are you grinning, skull?
You also tried for truth and lost your way?
You microscopes and test tubes,
You were supposed to be my key
But you never turned the lock.
Mysterious in broad daylight
Nature won't talk despite our demonstrations;
What she won't reveal to spirit
Will never be forced by screws and levers.
My father's alchemic texts – !
What you inherit's only loaned to you,
You have to use it to possess it,
What's not used is only an extra burden.
The present moment uses only what serves it.

That flask! Let me take you down devoutly,
Praise your essence of man's art and scope,
You summation of all sleeping pills,
Dancer of death's subtle counter-movements.
My time has come to attempt
New planes of pure activity!
Resolute, I turn my back on earth.
I'll fling open those gates
That most men slink by.
It's time for me to prove my courage
Equal to a god's,
Not let imagination keep me scared of death.
To resolutely, cheerfully take this step
Though total disappearance is the risk.
(Raises cup to lips.)
Youth! What did I do with my dreams?
Once I saw a universe,
True civilization,
Earth enhanced and glorified,
Truth in human form,
Beauty in a City,

Sacred Memory!
I remember now!
Earth, take back your son!
(Puts down cup.)
I shall call upon the supernatural
I must seek out revelation
In the highest source I know, John's Gospel.
I will determine its meaning
And translate it into my own language!
(Opens huge tome.)
It is written:
"In the beginning was the *Word*."
No, I cannot rate the *Word* so high
I must try a new translation
If the spirit's truly teaching me.
"In the beginning was the *Idea*."
Let me ponder this first line,
Not allow my pen to control me.
Is it *Mind* that works, creates, rules?
"In the beginning was the *Power*."
My fingers willing push the pen,
But have I fully tested the meaning?
The spirit sees my need,
"In the beginning was the *Deed*."

MEPHISTOPHELES
(Dressed as a travelling scholar. Knocks. Enters.)
Maybe I can help you, sir.

FAUST
You, a travelling scholar, help me?
What a laugh!

MEPHISTOPHELES
I bow before such a learned man.

FAUST
Your name?

MEPHISTOPHELES
That question hardly seems worthy
Of a man who rates the *Word* so low,
Who has no love for appearances
And values only essence.

FAUST
The nature of you dubious types
Is often revealed by your name
As for example Beelzebub, The Lord of Flies.
Well, who are you?

MEPHISTOPHELES
Part of that power
That always wills evil
But is forced to work the good.

FAUST
Explain your riddle.

MEPHISTOPHELES
I am the spirit that denies
And rightly denies,
For all created component things
Born from the void
Are fit only for destruction.
It would be better if creation stopped.
So all that you call downfall, ruin,
Catastrophe, sin, is what I revel in.

FAUST
You call yourself part of a Power,
Yet you appear complete?

MEPHISTOPHELES
In modesty, I speak the truth.
Let man, that vain fool,

Brag about being a microcosmos, whole.
Part of a part am I,
A part of Darkness that once was All
Until she brought forth Light,
Light that seeks to rule all space
And eliminate the mother Darkness.
But Light's empire is doomed,
Light cannot escape from material forms,
Light comes from matter, beautifies matter,
Is absorbed by matter, and so must
Dissolve with matter into nothing.

FAUST

A noble plan!
You can't wreck everything at once,
So you begin wherever you can.

MEPHISTOPHELES

Frankly, I still don't accomplish much.
Annihilation's denial meets assertion
Inspiring all these coarse component things.
I've used earthquake, hurricane, volcano –
Sea and continent amiably adjust themselves.
And that damned brood of men and beasts –
What's the use to play with that?
I bury millions every year
Yet there's more and yet more
Young, fresh, circulating blood!
It makes me mad
To see from earth and air and water
All those seeds and germs advance
Through drought and flood, ice age and tropic.
Fire is mine, the power of fire,
And nothing else to call my own.

FAUST

So, against immortal Creative Power

You rage and raise your hand?
Strange unprofitable son of Chaos
Why don't you find some more hopeful enterprise?

MEPHISTOPHELES
Well, we can talk about that later.
I'd like to leave for now, please.

FAUST
We're acquaintances, now, why ask?
Just use the door.

MEPHISTOPHELES
There's a small problem.
That yantra above your door.

FAUST
My pentagram!
If that keeps you from going out
How did you get in?

MEPHISTOPHELES
Examine your work!
You didn't quite finish the outer angle,
The lines don't meet.

FAUST
So luck has made you my prisoner!

MEPHISTOPHELES
The wandering scholar danced blindly in.
Now it's serious. The devil can't get out.

FAUST
How about the window?

MEPHISTOPHELES
We devils must obey a certain law.

The way we enter, we must leave by.
Free to enter, we're governed by our exits.

FAUST
Hell itself must follow rules and regulations!
Good, with law we can making binding contracts,
So why not negotiate with the devil?

MEPHISTOPHELES
What the devil promises shall delight you.
And we're not double-dealing tightwads.
But deals like this take time,
We'll talk about it later.
Right now, please, let me leave.

FAUST
Stay a little longer.
Tell me something about the future.

MEPHISTOPHELES
Let me go. I'll come back soon,
Then you can question me at will.

FAUST
I didn't ask you to come.
You trapped yourself –
When you catch a devil, hold him!
It's hard to catch one twice.

MEPHISTOPHELES
Since you wish, I'm glad to stay
And keep you company
But I must stipulate that I use my arts.

FAUST
Willingly! if you can amuse me.

MEPHISTOPHELES

This hour, friend, will rouse your senses
More than a year in your dull routine.
What shall be sung to you
Will set your subtle feelings all aglow.
I don't need the paraphernalia.
Begin!

SPIRITS

One Two Three
Can't you see
You are free
Dance and sing
Follow the sun
Stand on a peak
Find what you seek
Tear down your bars
You're with the stars
Your shadow's the moon
Howl with the loon
Dive in the lake
Your thirst slake
Go on the make
Take Take Take
Fly through the air
Jewels in your lair
Up or down
Go out on the town
Everything's doing
Beauty's renewing
The galaxies want you
All your wishes are true!

MEPHISTOPHELES

You've put him asleep.
Well done, boys, well done
And I thank you.

Professor, you're not the man to trap the devil.
Hold him there with dreams and images
He prefers the oceans of sweet illusion.
Now to break his spell,
I need a rat's tooth.
I hear one rustle; he'll do.
  The King of Rats and Mice
  Flies, Bugs, Frogs and Lice
  Commands you to door.
  To work! Chew his lore.
  Another bite!
The pentagram's crunched.
Dream on, Faust, till we meet again.

Scene 2

(Faust's study. Knocking.)

FAUST
Come in! Who disturbs my quiet?

MEPHISTOPHELES
It's I.

FAUST
Come in!

MEPHISTOPHELES
I wait for the third request.

FAUST
Come in, then.

MEPHISTOPHELES
That's how to welcome friends.

And I hope our friendship grows.
To drive away your headaches
I come dressed as a revolutionary artist,
With a pistol for use or show,
And I advise you to do the same,
Then with the freedom that the devil gives,
Life will be revealed to you at last.

FAUST

I don't care how I'd dress up;
Life on earth's imprisoning, painful, lonely.
I'm too old to play,
Too young to have lost desire.
What can I get from the world?
You shall renounce, give up, stop!
We're told this, again and again and again.
Our entire lives, over and over and over.
Each morning I wake up in terror,
It makes me cry to see the sun
Knowing that by night not one of my longings,
Not one, will come true;
To see each beginning joy destroyed by doubt,
To see each creative effort
Mocked, ignored, spurned by the life around me.
At night I don't get sleep,
Wild dreams shatter me.
The god within whips me to a storm,
But though all my faculties are aroused,
He gives no power to command external forces.
Thus, life's taught me with weary lessons
To long for death and hold living at a distance.

MEPHISTOPHELES

But I doubt that death's ever welcome.

FAUST

Happy the soldier who dies in victory;

Happy the dancer dying upon his girl;
I wish I could die in samadhi, ecstatic.

MEPHISTOPHELES
Yet you didn't drink your poison.

FAUST
So, you're an eavesdropper as well?

MEPHISTOPHELES
I'm not omniscient, but I am well-informed.

FAUST
Some old associative train of romantic images
Deceived me, a left-over faith of childhood.
But now I curse whatever tempts the soul with dreams,
And causes it to linger in this painful body;
I curse ambition that deludes the mind;
I curse illusions that annoint our senses;
I curse honor, that cheating word;
I curse fame that blinds us to time's executions;
I curse the flattery of possessing
Wife, child, land, machines;
I curse money that spurs us to restless actions;
I curse money that indulges us to loaf;
I curse wine's transcendent lure;
I curse Love's finest dance;
I curse Hope, curse Faith,
And curse Patience most of all!

SPIRIT CHORUS
(Invisible)
Doom! Doom!
You have destroyed
A beautiful world
With relentless hand,
Hurled it in ruins,

A demigod in despair!
We carry its scattered fragments
Into the void
Mourning
Beauty smashed beyond repair.
Magician,
Mightiest of men,
Raise your world
More splendid than before,
From your heart's blood
Build it up again!
Create a new cycle
For the splendors of sense to adorn;
You'll hear life
Chant a new and fresher song.

MEPHISTOPHELES
These friends of mine
Urge you back to deeds and joy.
Back into the struggle
Out of this lonely madness
That betrays your flesh and blood.
Give up your suffering
That eats your mind.
No matter how stupid the crowd
It'll cheer you up, show you you're a man.
Of course, I don't mean
To put you on Skid Road or in the masses;
I'm not the emperor or pope,
But if you'll take me as your guide,
I'll serve you very well, your slave.

FAUST
What will I have to pay?

MEPHISTOPHELES
Oh, you can find out later.

FAUST

No, no. The devil's an egotist.
You don't help me for the love of God or man.
State your conditions exactly.

MEPHISTOPHELES

Then *here*, I work for you,
Obedient even to your whims.
If we happen to meet *there*,
You'll do the same for me.

FAUST

The *other* doesn't scare me.
After you've destroyed this world,
Let the *other* come.
It's from this earth my joys rise,
This sun contemplates my sorrows,
If my life leaves these,
Well, let happen what happens.
I'm tired of listening to cowards
Calculate if we shall love or hate
Or if there's an Above or a Below.

MEPHISTOPHELES

Right on. That's the spirit for adventure.
Now, let's draw up our deal.
I will show you the arts of ecstasy.
You shall see what no man has ever seen.

FAUST

What can you, poor devil, give me?
When was a human soul on its supreme search
Ever understood by the likes of you?
Your bread never transubstantiates;
It always leaves us hungry.
Your gold flows through our hands like water.
Only losers have ever played your games.

The girls you give, even while in our arms,
Are already flirting with our neighbor.
Your dreams of destiny burn out like meteors.
You must show me trees and shrubs
That change their leaves and flowers daily!

MEPHISTOPHELES
That I can and will show you.
But let's also peacefully relish forbidden treasures.

FAUST
That moment I relax on your bed of roses,
That moment take my life!
If your lying flattery ever makes me self-satisfied,
If you make me a slave of pleasure,
Take my soul, I desire to die.
I'll bet you that.

MEPHISTOPHELES
Done!

FAUST
And willingly!
If ever I plead with the fleeting moment
"Linger, linger, you are so beautiful",
Take me as your slave, kill me,
Ring out my death chimes to free yourself,
And time finished off for me.

MEPHISTOPHELES
Remember, I don't forget.

FAUST
Don't worry,
I'm not manufacturing rhetoric.
If I get that fascinated by images, I'm a slave,
I don't care if yours or whose I am.

MEPHISTOPHELES

I'll start tonight at your doctoral banquet.
But as insurance – give me a line in writing.

FAUST

You also want a document, you bureaucrat?
You've never heard of a man keeping his word?
Civilizations and nations pass away,
And you think my promise dubious.
Happy is the man who keeps his faith,
Never will he regret himself.
Still, a legal paper, signed and sealed
Works witchcraft on the strongest men.
The word dies in the drying ink,
And paper lords it over kings and sages.
Therefore, devil, do you prefer paper, marble, brass?
Shall I write with pen, chisel or graver?
I give you your choice. Take your pick!

MEPHISTOPHELES

Don't overwork your rhetoric.
Any scrap of paper's fine.
To sign it, use a drop of blood.

FAUST

If this satisfies you, I'll play out the farce.

MEPHISTOPHELES

Blood is a juice of rare quality.

FAUST

Don't be afraid I'll run out on this contract.
All my strength shall go into this bet.
My self-love made me imagine greatness,
But I'm clearly on your level.
Spirit has never given me free and open answer,
And even Nature keeps her mystery.

My train of thought is shattered,
I'm disgusted with learning's pretensions.
Let's put out the pain of passion's fire;
Bring out your marveled sensual delights,
Make magic wonders right out front.
From fake eternity I plunge into time's dance,
Bob up and down on waves of circumstance!
Bring pain or pleasure, triumph or disaster,
To evolve, man needs necessity.

MEPHISTOPHELES
Enjoy what you want, money, pleasure, beauty.
Fall to, plunder the universe, don't be coy!

FAUST
You didn't hear me. Joy's not the point.
I take the karmic cycle, organic pain,
Love-hate, exultant agony.
My heart, liberated from books and lectures,
Does not wish any sort of monastery,
But to share the total human hazard.
There's no height, no depth, I won't explore;
I'll entwine myself with every soul,
Share the total shipwreck of humanity.

MEPHISTOPHELES
Listen, for thousands of years, I've chewed this meat;
No man has digested the whole from birth to death.
This sense of unity is for a god alone.
In supernal light, *He* sees the Whole,
But *us*, he pushes into the dark,
And to *you*, he gives alternating day and night.

FAUST
My mind's made up. I will.

MEPHISTOPHELES
Good. Good. Well said.

Yet art is long and time disappears.
You'd better go find a poet-teacher,
Apprentice yourself to his imagination,
Let him reveal to you the secret and the glory
That bind light and dark together,
Teach you to blend cleverness with magnanimity,
To love passionately, but with objective plan.
Ha! I'd like to see this paragon myself.
Sir Microcosm I'd call him.

FAUST
What am I, then,
If I can't become what man should be,
That for which even my senses pray?

MEPHISTOPHELES
You, when all is said and done, are what you are.
Put on a wig, walk on stilts, make-up your face,
You remain exactly what you are.

FAUST
I know. I'm Doctor, Professor, Scientist.
But the moment I rest a second,
I see I'm nowhere near the source.
I'm not a half-inch taller,
Nor any nearer to the infinite.

MEPHISTOPHELES
Now you see the facts precisely –
As everybody sees them.
You must learn to be more clever.
Why, your hands, feet, head and ass are yours,
And the things we use, aren't they ours, too?
If I've horse or car, isn't their strength mine?
So divorce sterile reason and empty meditation.
Let's take on the world!
Grey are all theories,
The tree of life alone is green.

FAUST

Allright. How should we begin?

MEPHISTOPHELES

By dropping out of this university.
Man, what a martyrdom!
Is it life, I ask you, is it even safe
To bore yourself and bore your students?
Leave that to fat guts, fat asses and fat heads.
Even if you ever learned something,
You'd be fired for telling youth!
Quick! Go change your clothes!
(Faust leaves.)
The Prince of Lies will teach you
With magic works and shows.
I'll get him.
Fate gave him such free, wild spirit
That forward, onward, upward, downward,
He's driven past earth's joy and natural law.
I'll drag him through the savage gutter,
Through acts of stifling insignificance.
He'll find the deal he hassled leaves him writhing.
The dreams I conjure will mock his appetite,
He'll cry like a child for comfort.
Nothing can save him now.
His soul's destroyed forever!

Scene 3

(Auerbach's wine-cellar. Leipzig.)

FROSCH

Nobody's laughing! Nobody's drinking!
How come you're all so dull and grim?
This is supposed to be where the action's at,

Blazing like a bonfire,
But you're a bunch of wet blankets.

BRANDER
You're the cause yourself.
You're not telling stories or acting up.

FROSCH
(Empties wine glass on Brander's head.)
How's that for a start?

BRANDER
You swine!

FROSCH
You asked for it!

SIEBEL
Can't take a joke?
Bouncer! Bounce him out!
Let's sing and shout.
Swine and swill, buddies,
And shout it out!
Hey! Ho! Ho! Hey! Ha! Ha! Ho!

ALTMAYER
Cotton! Cotton for my ears!
You bellow like a wounded bull!

SIEBEL
It's when a man's voice shakes the rafters
That you know he has a bass.

FROSCH
Hear, hear!
Throw anybody out who gets uptight.
Ya-da-da-da-duh!

ALTMAYER
Ya-da-da-da-duh!

FROSCH
Everybody's throat tuned-up? Begin!
The Empire, the good old Empire,
What keeps it going?

BRANDER
A dirty song! A political song!
A lousy song! Thank God continually
That you're not responsible for the state.
I thank my lucky stars, and know I'm smarter,
Not to be the president or kaiser.
But we also should have a leader
So let's choose ourselves a pope.
Let the best man win,
And he can lead our drinking!

FROSCH
(Singing)
Love, love, beautiful love,
Bow down to my sweetheart.

SIEBEL
Down with love-songs, too!
Who cares about your sweetheart?

FROSCH
I'll sing about love and kisses anyhow.
Open the door, it's late.
Open, don't make your lover wait.
Close the door and steal away.

SIEBEL
Sing on, sing on and brag,
It'll soon be my turn to laugh,

She led me by the nose and she's got you.
Stinking he-goats from a witches' sabbath
Would be plenty fine for her.
A fellow of flesh and blood's too good
For that double-crossing wench.
The only song she'd make me perform
Would be the smashing of her windows!

BRANDER
(Pounding table.)
Order, order in the court!
Listen, men, I know how to live.
There's lovers here,
And manners means
I sing them something to the point.
You guys pick up the chorus.
Once in a basement lived a rat
Cheese and butter were his soother
His little paunch grew fat
As that of Doctor Luther.
But the cook put poison out.
Pain in his guts made him shout
That love consumes my vitals!

CHORUS
That love consumes my vitals!

BRANDER
He ran he jumped he lurched
He slurped at every puddle
But still his body scorched
More painful still his muddle.
The torment drove him mad
He shook and screamed as if he said
That love consumes my vitals!

CHORUS

That love consumes my vitals!

BRANDER

So panicked he forgot daylight
And ran into the kitchen
Flopped around, a deadly sight,
Soon was only twitching.
The cook laughed, she was so gay.
"If you were a poet, you'd say
That love consumes my vitals."

CHORUS

That love consumes my vitals!

SIEBEL

How can you enjoy that kind of wit?
It doesn't take much skill
To poison some poor rat!

BRANDER

Hey, hey! He's a rat-lover!

CHORUS

That love consumes *his* vitals!

ALTMAYER

Look at the bald potbelly!
Look at his face.
When the rat bloats with poison
He sees a member of *his* race!

(Enter Faust and Mephistopheles.)

MEPHISTOPHELES

Before anything else, I bring you here
To see how boon companions laugh together,

To see how life can be all play.
For these people, each day's a holiday.
Not too bright but completely at their ease,
They play like kittens with their own tail,
And barring hangovers from the night before,
And as long as their credit holds good,
They haven't a care in the world.

BRANDER
These two are travelers,
You can see that by the way they dress.
Just arrived in town, I'd guess.

FROSCH
You're right. That's why I like it here in Leipzig.
Our town's a little Paris, almost a cultural center.

SIEBEL
What do you think they do?

FROSCH
Leave it to me.
After a glass or two
I'll extract their secrets like milk teeth.
You can see they're of the upper class,
But discontented rebels by their artist's dress.

BRANDER
Quack doctors peddling lady's cures, I bet.

ALTMAYER
You may be right.

FROSCH
Watch how I smoke them out.

MEPHISTOPHELES
Even if I had them by the neck

These fellows would never sniff the devil.

FAUST
Good evening, friends.

SIEBEL
Same to you.
(Whispers) That fellow's lame in one foot.

MEPHISTOPHELES
Do you mind if we join your little party?
Companionship is very welcome
When the wine's so poor.

ALTMAYER
You're very persnickety.

FROSCH
You must have left Rippach fairly late.
Probably ate at Otto's for dinner?

MEPHISTOPHELES
We didn't stop today,
But last time had quite a talk.
He spoke about his cousins
And said we should say hello to each.
(Bows to Frosch.)

ALTMAYER
(Whispers)
He's on to you!

SIEBEL
Sharp as a tack.

FROSCH
Wait a while – I'll catch him off guard.

MEPHISTOPHELES
But didn't I hear some singing,
Well-trained voices, a real quartet;
Yes, song must echo beautifully
From this vaulted roof.

FROSCH
You are a real hotshot?

MEPHISTOPHELES
No, no. My desire is great, my capacity so-so.

ALTMAYER
Sing us something!

MEPHISTOPHELES
As many as you like.

SIEBEL
Something new!

MEPHISTOPHELES
Nothing easier. We've just come back from Spain
That lovely land of wine and song and sleep.
Oh once there was a king
Who had a big black flea

FROSCH
Hear that? A flea! A lousy guest!

MEPHISTOPHELES
Oh once there was a king
Who had a big black flea
He loved him like anything,
Better than his son, loved he.
He called upon his tailor
His tailor came right away

"Make trousers for this sailor,
And a coat, right now, I say."

BRANDER

Don't let the tailor get away with anything.
Make him exactly measure, cut and sew.
There mustn't be a single wrinkle!

MEPHISTOPHELES

He gleamed in silk and velvet,
The flea was fully dressed,
He strutted up the carpet,
Medals upon his breast.
He filled the highest stations
Bought up a great estate
Promoted his poor relations
To shine among the great.
The Lords and Ladies groaned
In the park and in the bed
The Queen was bit and moaned
The maids were bit and bled.
They weren't allowed to scratch them
Or brush them off
But we can grab and scratch them
And brush or crush them off!

CHORUS

But we can grab and scratch them
And brush or crush them off!

FROSCH

Bravo! Bravo! That's the way to sing!

SIEBEL

Down with fleas!

BRANDER

Between your nails! Crack them in two!

ALTMAYER
A toast! To liberty! To wine!

MEPHISTOPHELES
I'd have a glass with you to freedom
But your local stuff's no good.

SIEBEL
Let's don't hear that again.

MEPHISTOPHELES
Well, if I didn't think the bartender would object
I'd offer each of you the best from my cellar.

SIEBEL
Just treat, I'll take care of the bartender.

FROSCH
If your wine's really good, we shall appreciate it.
But fill the glasses up
Because for me to judge its quality
I need a good mouthful.

ALTMAYER
They're from the Rhine, I knew it.

MEPHISTOPHELES
Give me a gimlet.

BRANDER
Why? You don't have casks outside the door?

ALTMAYER
There's one, hanging on that post.

MEPHISTOPHELES
(Takes gimlet. To Frosch:)
Now, what's your taste? Sparkling burgundy?

FROSCH
What do you mean? How many kinds do you have?

MPEHISTOPHELES
Any kind you want.

ALTMAYER
You're drooling like a dog.

FROSCH
Well, if I have to choose, Rhenish!
The Fatherland makes the best!

MEPHISTOPHELES
(Boring hole in table-edge, by Frosch.)
Wax, to make the stoppers, quick!

ALTMAYER
A magician's trick.

MEPHISTOPHELES
(To Brander:)
And yours?

BRANDER
Champagne. And let it foam and sparkle.
(Mephistopheles bores, Frosch plugs in wax stoppers.)
We don't need to always ban the foreign stuff.
Fine things aren't always found at home.
We Germans hate the French,
But their wines are pretty good.

SIEBEL
I prefer sweet wines.

MEPHISTOPHELES
Tokay for you! *(Bores at his place.)*

ALTMAYER

Come on, look me straight in the face.
You're making fun of us, or a silly joke.

MEPHISTOPHELES

A practical joke with gentlemen like you?
Not to be thought of.
Speak up, what's your choice?

ALTMAYER

I'm not particular. Let it flow!

MEPHISTOPHELES

(With full gestures.)

Grapes grow on the vine
He-goats' horns are fine
Wine from juice, grape from wood,
Table gives us wine as good.
Nature! Nature! We are here
Make a miracle appear!

ALL

(Drawing wine from the spigots.)

Watch it come! Watch it flow!

MEPHISTOPHELES

Don't spill any of it!

ALL

(Drinking wildly.)

Hell's dogs, we drink the wine
Happier than any swine,
Drink drink drink
And never think.

MEPHISTOPHELES

The barriers are down. Behold democracy!

FAUST

Let's go. I've had enough.

MEPHISTOPHELES

No, first watch the revelation of their bestiality.
(Siebel spills wine, that turns to fire on hitting floor.)

ALL

Help! Fire! Help! A Hellish Fire!

MEPHISTOPHELES
(Conjuring)

Quiet down, friendly element.
Don't worry. Only a sample of purgatory.

SIEBEL

We'll make you pay for that.
Who do you think we are to try such games?

FROSCH

Don't try that a second time.

ALTMAYER

I think you'd better split.

SIEBEL

How dare you try your hocus-pocus here?

MEPHISTOPHELES

Shut up, wine barrel.

SIEBEL

You think you can add insult to injury?

BRANDER

He's asking for it! Slug him!

ALTMAYER
(Draws from his plug. A spurt of fire.)
Fire, fire!

SIEBEL
This is magic! He's an outlaw!
Draw your knives! Cut him down!

MEPHISTOPHELES
Word, time and space
Be all confounded
Lose all sense of place!

ALTMAYER
Where am I? What a lovely land!

FROSCH
Vineyards everywhere.

SIEBEL
Clusters of grapes!

BRANDER
Look at the grapes ready for the cutting!
(He takes Siebel by the nose, all do the same, and raise their knives.)

MEPHISTOPHELES
Illusion, disappear!
See the Devil's jeer! *(He disappears with Faust.)*

SIEBEL
What happened?

ALTMAYER
Yes, what?

FROSCH
I held your nose.

BRANDER
And, Siebel, I'm still holding yours.

ALTMAYER
That was a shock!
Give me a chair. I'm dizzy.

FROSCH
Just what really happened?

SIEBEL
Where is he? If I got my hands on him,
That'd be the end.

ALTMAYER
I saw him riding out the door,
Flying on a wine cask.
My feet are weighted down.
I wonder if the table still gives wine?

SIEBEL
It was all lies, a sleight of hand.

FROSCH
It looked like wine and tasted good.

BRANDER
What about the grapes we tried to cut?

ALTMAYER
Maybe miracles still occur.

Scene 4

(Witches kitchen. A huge cauldron over a fire. A She-ape tends the cauldron. A He-ape lolligags.)

FAUST
Going to a witch disgusts my soul!
How can this old hag
Take thirty years off my age?
This is the best you can do?
Why hasn't a noble mind invented something better?

MEPHISTOPHELES
There is another recipe,
But I doubt it'd do you any good.

FAUST
Tell me.

MEPHISTOPHELES
Allright. You don't need money, doctor or magic.
Go to the country. Grow your own food.
Eat pure organic vegetables.
Live with the cattle like one of them,
And manure your own garden.
For eighty years you'll keep your youth.

FAUST
That life's too limited for me.

MEPHISTOPHELES
Therefore we call on the witch.

FAUST
Why can't you do it yourself?

MEPHISTOPHELES
I've got a thousand things to do.

Art and science aren't enough;
This job takes patience, too.
Time alone can work this brew.
The ingredients are rare and strange.
The devil taught her how,
But the devil cannot make it.

FAUST
(Gazing into a mirror.)
What a beautiful woman!
I never dreamed one could be so lovely!
Can such a one exist on earth?

MEPHISTOPHELES
Of course. When a god works six days,
Cries bravo at his work, and takes a day off,
There ought to be something to show for it.
I'll find you a beauty as voluptuous,
Make her yours,
And you can happily teach her love.

WITCH
(Enters)
Ai-ee! Ai-ee! Ai-ee!
Who are you?
What do you want?
Sneaky dogs,
Roast with hogs!
(She throws scald from the cauldron at them.)

MEPHISTOPHELES
I'll break your pots
With magic shots;
I'll fix your hash
Crash crash crash.
I beat time,
You sing the tune.

(Witch retreats in hate.)
Bag of bones, don't you recognize your lord and master?
What keeps me from annihilating you
And your monkeys?
Don't I have the same face,
Do I have to introduce myself, garlic breath?

WITCH
Pardon me, but where is your cloven foot,
And your two black ravens?

MEPHISTOPHELES
This time I'll let you off
Since we haven't met for a century.
Society's learned to read and write,
And even culture's gone to the devil.
Horns and tail and claws are out of style,
The Northern spook is dead.

WITCH
(Dancing)
Sense and reason go!
My Satan's here again!

MEPHISTOPHELES
That name's also out.

WITCH
Why?

MEPHISTOPHELES
Men are too enlightened now.
They laugh at the Evil *ONE*
And struggle with the Evil *MANY*.
Call me Mister! *(Indecent gesture.)*

WITCH
(Laughing)
That's still you!
A rogue you were, a rogue you are.

MEPHISTOPHELES
My friend, observe how to handle witches.

WITCH
Now, tell me, how can I help you?

MEPHISTOPHELES
A glass of your famous brew.
Well aged so its strength is certain.

WITCH
Gladly. Here's a bottle I use myself.
So old it no longer stinks.
(Whisper) But if he's not prepared, it's sure psychosis.

MEPHISTOPHELES
He's my friend. Don't worry.
Draw your circle. Pronounce your charms.
And fill his glass.
(The Witch makes her circle; arranges the Apes,
beckons to Faust.)

FAUST
Why does she parade her booklearning?
I've seen these diagrams, read these words,
And know that charlatans use them.

MEPHISTOPHELES
Of course it's nonsense.
But it knocks sobersidedness out of you,
And loosens you up to receive the drug.
(Gets Faust into circle.)

WITCH
(Reading from a book.)

Learn how to do;
Make one into ten;
Transcend two;
Three's the way in;
Now you're rich!
Word of a Witch!
Go past four
Five and six pour
Out seven and eight;
Complete your fate;
For nine makes one
And ten is none;
The Magic One times One!

FAUST

She's crazy.

MEPHISTOPHELES

You'll hear more. I know this book.
So full of paradox it traps the idiots and wise,
Ages have been taught these forms,
And men do three for one and one for three
Promoting error in the name of sacred truth.
They teach and rave; nobody stops them.
If men hear a high sounding word
They believe there must be meaning.

WITCH

The high skill
Of art and will
Is deeply hidden.
Who conquers thought,
It comes unsought,
Given unbidden.

FAUST

Nonsense! My head's splitting.
I hear a hundred thousand fools in chorus.

MEPHISTOPHELES

Sybil, leave off. Bring out your stuff.
Fill his goblet right to the brim.
He won't get hurt;
He's experimented with a hundred drugs.
(The Witch ceremoniously pours.)

MEPHISTOPHELES

Down it, man, never hesitate!
It'll make your body glow with new desire.
You call yourself the devil's friend?
And flinch before a witch's goblet?
(Witch dissolves circle. Faust steps out.)
Let's go. You mustn't rest.

WITCH

May you profit from the drink.

MEPHISTOPHELES
(To Witch:)

Tell me what you wish on Walpurgis Night
And you shall have it.

WITCH

Here's a text for you to sing at proper times.

MEPHISTOPHELES

Never mind. You have to work up a sweat
And drive the drug throughout your body.
I'll teach you how to live,
And you'll see, with thrills of pleasure,
How your attention's riveted by Woman.

FAUST
Let me look in that mirror again.

MEPHISTOPHELES
You don't need a mirror now. That beauty
You'll soon see in the flesh.
(Aside) With a dose like that
Every skirt will hold Helen of Troy!

Scene 5

(A street. Faust. Margareta passes by.)

FAUST
May I offer you my arm, fair lady,
And escort you home?

MARGARETA
My title's not that of lady, I'm not fair,
And I don't need an escort to find my way home.
(Frees her arm and leaves.)

FAUST
That girl – beauty!
Exquisite, enchanting, good,
But with saucy wit, and lively.
Time can't make me forget her eyes,
How she turned them down so tenderly,
Unlocking a pattern in my soul.
And her speech so short and sharp,
Quintessence of the charm of youth!
(Enter Mephistopheles.)
Listen, that's the girl I want to have.

MEPHISTOPHELES
What girl?

FAUST
That one – that just walked by.

MEPHISTOPHELES
That girl? She's coming from confession
Where the priest absolved all her sins,
But actually I was eavesdropping,
And I can tell you she had nothing to confess.
She's innocence itself;
The devil has no power over one that pure.

FAUST
She's over fourteen, isn't she?

MEPHISTOPHELES
You've become quite the libertine, haven't you?
You think each flower's for you to pluck,
That nothing's beyond your reach,
But you'll have to learn
That nobody can make everyone.

FAUST
Listen, professor,
I don't want to hear you moralize.
I want that sweet young girl
In my arms tonight –
Or our bargain's off – at twelve o'clock!

MEPHISTOPHELES
Consider the parameters of the problem –
I need at least two weeks
To set up the time and place.

FAUST
Give me seven hours with the girl,
I wouldn't need your help
But would seduce her all alone.

MEPHISTOPHELES

In one day you're talking like a Frenchman!
But I advise a profounder strategy,
You'll get much more pleasure
If you caress and lead her on awhile,
Mold and shape her to your wish
Just as Italian stories teach.

FAUST

My appetite's already up.

MEPHISTOPHELES

I've joked with you long enough.
I tell you once and for all
You can't just push that lovely girl upon her back.
You'll only lose by using force
You must use cunning here.

FAUST

Get me something she wears.
Take me to her bedroom!
Get me the handkerchief between her breasts,
Or the slip that clothes her hips.

MEPHISTOPHELES

I'll prove my loyalty to your passion.
I'll find and take you to her room.

FAUST

Shall I see her, take her?

MEPHISTOPHELES

No, she's visiting a neighbor.
But you can breathe in her aura,
And dwell upon her ravishing.

FAUST

Can we go now?

MEPHISTOPHELES
It's too early yet.

FAUST
Prepare the best gift money can buy. *(Leaves)*

MEPHISTOPHELES
Presents right away? He'll make her.
That's the best, easiest and cleverest way.
I know lots of buried treasure.
I'll go sort some baubles out.

Scene 6

(Evening. Small, neat room.)

MARGARETA
(Brushing her hair.)
I wish I knew who he was.
A free and creative man –
I could read that much in his face –
Otherwise he could never have been so daring.
(Leaves. Faust and Mephistopheles enter.)

MEPHISTOPHELES
Come on in, but quietly.

FAUST
Leave me alone. I'll see you later.

MEPHISTOPHELES
Not every girl keeps things so neat. *(Leaves)*

FAUST
Here is the atmosphere of contentment.

Not much money, but full of love.
This little room breathes perfect happiness.
Dear girl, your spirit enchants my soul.
Your capable and careful hand
Has made a cottage into a lower heaven.
Your bed! Ecstasy pulses in my blood.
I could dream many hours away –
How the child lay here through essence nights,
How her breasts warmed with the life-force.
And I? With what purpose did I come?
Miserable Faust, you've changed!
What a magic spirit's here.
I came on fire for lust's instant pleasure,
And now I want true love!
With every breath we change our thoughts!
If she entered now, what would I do?
The braggart would fall at her feet, ashamed.

MEPHISTOPHELES
Quick! She's at the corner.

FAUST
Let's go! And I won't come back.

MEPHISTOPHELES
Here's a jewel casket, good and heavy;
Lay it on her dresser. Hurry!
It'll turn her head to see it.
There's enough there to get two girls.
A girl's a girl, and love's – love.

FAUST
Will I, or won't I?

MEPHISTOPHELES
What's the matter with you?
You want the jewels for yourself?

Then please don't waste my time
And profane the name of lust by greed.
(He locks casket in chest.)
Now, let's get out of here.
I'm racking my brains studying your desires.

MARGARETA
(Enters)
It's so close and sultry. *(Opens window.)*
Yet it's cool outside.
I feel a kind of fear. Where's mother?
I'm a silly to shudder so. *(Begins to undress, singing.)*

In Thule there ruled a king
Faithful unto death.
His mistress gave him a goblet
And then gave God her breath.

This golden cup he loved,
He drank from it alone,
And every time he drank
His tears were newly shown.

It came his time to die
His mighty wealth was told
He left his son his treasure
Except the cup of gold.

He proclaimed a royal feast
Invited all of high degree
To his father's father's castle
That loomed above the sea.

That ancient king stood up,
Drank his life's last glow,
Then hurled his sacred goblet
Into the waves below.

He watched it slowly fill
And sink into the sea,
The light forsook his eyes,
And never again drank he.

(She opens dresser to put away clothes. Sees casket.)
Where did this lovely casket come from?
I know I locked the dresser.
Maybe it's a security
Against a loan my mother made.
There's a key on the ribbon.
I'll open it just once and look.
Dear God! How lovely!
These jewels are fit for the Duchess
To wear on the Court's holiday.
How would this necklace look on me?
I wonder whose these are.
(She adorns herself. Looks in mirror.)
I wish I owned these earrings.
Beauty is not enough for a girl.
Men may say "How young, how lovely,"
But there's a touch of pity in their praise
Of any girl that has no money.
The power of gold
The magic of gold!
Alas, we poor!

Scene 7

(A walk. Faust paces to and fro. Mephistopheles joins him.)

MEPHISTOPHELES
By love that's mocked! By Hell's tortures!
If I knew anything worse
I'd swear by it.

FAUST
What's eating you?
I never saw a face like yours.

MEPHISTOPHELES
I'd give myself to the devil
If I weren't already the devil!

FAUST
It doesn't suit you to rave like this.

MEPHISTOPHELES
A priest! A priest got Margareta's jewels!
Her mother saw them; her conscience acted up.
She's always nosing troubles out;
Always sniffing in her prayer books;
She even smells everything she buys
To see if they're genuine or synthetic.
To the jewelry she gives one whiff
And her suspicion's up.
"My child," she cries, "stolen goods
Will ruin your soul and life.
We'll give this to the Blessed Mary
And she'll repay our souls with interest."
But Margareta thought "A gift!"
And "No giver such as this is godless!"
The mother called the priest immediately.
He saw the possibilities at once.
"My daughter," he says, "overcome the flesh to win.
The Church alone can swallow lands and gold,
And never overeat.
The Church alone
Has the digestion for stolen goods."

FAUST
The state and banker also practice this.

MEPHISTOPHELES
He sweeps all the necklaces, rings, bracelets
Into his bag like a woman at a store,
Thanks them as if for a bag of nuts,
Promised them full payment in Heaven –
They felt deeply edified.

FAUST
And Margareta?

MEPHISTOPHELES
Discontented. Won't resent and can't forget.
Dreams of the splendid casket,
But even more of the man who gave it.

FAUST
I don't want her to grieve!
Get another set for her!
The first could be improved.

MEPHISTOPHELES
Children want their toys fixed, right now!

FAUST
Do as I say!
Get in with her neighbor,
And another casket for my love!

MEPHISTOPHELES
Yes, sir! *(Faust leaves.)*
Fools in love would blow up the planets
To give his darling a diverting show.

Scene 8

(Neighbor's house.)

MARTHA

God forgive my husband
Who ran off one day
Leaving me alone in bed.
I never crossed him,
I loved him, and can't forget him. *(Weeps)*
Maybe he's already dead –

MARGARETA

Martha!

MARTHA

What is it?

MARGARETA

It's unbelievable,
Another casket, this time ebony.
And jewels more splendid than the others!

MARTHA

Don't tell your mother
Or the priest will get it, too.

MARGARETA

Just look at them! Look!

MARTHA

(Putting jewelry on Margareta.)

How happy you are!

MARGARETA

But I don't dare wear them to town or to mass.

MARTHA

You can visit me more often,
Dress up, walk in front of the mirror,
We'll both enjoy it.
Then feasts and holidays will come;
Piece by piece you bring them out;
First a necklace, then pearls for your ears.
I'll find a story for your mother.

MARGARETA

But who's bringing me these gifts?
There must be something wrong –
(Knock) Oh, I hope that's not my mother.

MARTHA
(Peeping)

A man I've never seen before. Come in!

MEPHISTOPHELES

Thank you. I hope you'll excuse my boldness.
I'm looking for Martha Schwerdtlein.

MARTHA

That's me. What do you want?

MEPHISTOPHELES

Enough that you are she.
Since you've a noble visitor,
Pardon my intrusion. I'll come back later.

MARTHA

Well, I never! He thinks you're nobility!

MARGARETA

I'm only a poor young girl.
You're kind, but these jewels aren't mine.

MEPHISTOPHELES
Not the jewelry alone!
Your looks, your manners –
But I'm happy that I can stay.

MARTHA
What is your business?

MEPHISTOPHELES
I wish it was cheerful.
I hope you won't blame me.
Your husband's dead.

MARTHA
Dead? My dear husband!
What can I do now?

MARGARETA
Martha, don't give way.

MEPHISTOPHELES
And let me tell you the story.

MARGARETA
That's why I do not wish to love;
To lose my lover would be my death.

MEPHISTOPHELES
Every joy has its sorrow; that's the law of life.

MARTHA
Tell me how his life ended.

MEPHISTOPHELES
We buried him in Padua at St. Anthony's.
His grave well-consecrated for eternal rest.

MARTHA
He asked you to do nothing more?

MEPHISTOPHELES
One thing. To buy him three hundred masses,
To save his soul from Hell.
And that took all his money.

MARTHA
What? Not one lucky coin?
Not one ring, not one keepsake?

MEPHISTOPHELES
I'm very sorry, but he did use it well;
And his sins bothered, his bad luck tortured him.

MARGARETA
That men have such bad fortune!
I will pray for his soul's sake.

MEPHISTOPHELES
A girl so compassionate
Deserves a wedding!

MARGARETA
Marry? Not for many years.

MEPHISTOPHELES
If you don't marry, take a lover.
It's Heaven's greatest gift
To caress a dear one in the night.

MARGARETA
Our customs don't allow that, sir.

MEPHISTOPHELES
Custom or not, it happens all the same.

MARTHA
What else happened?

MEPHISTOPHELES
I watched him die upon a bed of stone.
He died a Christian, regretting his sins.
"I detest myself!" he cried.
"I deserted my wife, my home, my craft!
I pray that she forgives me!"

MARTHA
Dear man, I forgave him long ago.

MEPHISTOPHELES
"But God knows she was more to blame than I."

MARTHA
A lie! He lied on his death bed!

MEPHISTOPHELES
A man's senses rave in his death agony.
He said, "I lost my freedom and my play.
I first begot children, then I begot bread,
I worked years and years for bread
But happiness I never got."

MARTHA
Did he forget all my love and faith?
How I also worked day and night?

MEPHISTOPHELES
Not so. He remembered very well.
He said, "As our ship left Malta,
I prayed for wife and children.
Heaven answered right away.
We found and boarded a Turkish ship
Loaded with the Sultan's gold.

Then, since bravery was paid for,
I, quite justly, made a small fortune."

MARTHA
Where is it? Buried? Did he say?

MEPHISTOPHELES
Who knows? Blown to the four winds.
A young girl fell for him
As he wandered through Naples, friendless.
And she loved him so deeply,
He returned it to his dying day.

MARTHA
To rob his children and his wife!
Even his bad luck didn't wake him up!

MEPHISTOPHELES
That's true. No doubt that's why he's dead.
If I were in your place, I'd mourn a year,
Keeping a lookout for another mate.

MARTHA
It'd be hard to find another one like him.
The world's not overstocked with men.
He was a sweet and tender fool,
But he liked to travel,
Loved foreign women and foreign wine,
And loved to gamble most of all.

MEPHISTOPHELES
Well, well, that might've been quite allright,
If he'd let you do the same.
With that deal, I myself would marry you.

MARTHA
You're only joking, of course.

MEPHISTOPHELES
(Aside)
I think I'll get out of here.
This one would take the devil at his word!
(To Margareta:) What are you feeling?

MARGARETA
What do you mean?

MEPHISTOPHELES
Ah, you're an innocent charmer.
Ladies, farewell.

MARGARETA
Goodbye!

MARTHA
Wait a minute!
I need a legal witness to state
Where and how he died, where he was buried.
I like these things done right;
I want to read his obituary in the Sunday paper.

MEPHISTOPHELES
Two witnesses, Madam, establish truth.
Fortunately, I have a respected friend
Who will add his word to mine,
May I bring him here?

MARTHA
Please do.

MEPHISTOPHELES
And the young lady will be here, too?
He's a gallant lad, well-travelled;
Ladies always delight in him.

MARGARETA
I'd be too bashful to look at him.

MEPHISTOPHELES
Don't worry! You're fit for a king!

MARTHA
Tonight, in my little garden, then,
Behind the house, we'll expect the gentlemen.

Scene 9

(A street. Faust and Mephistopheles.)

FAUST
How's it going?

MEPHISTOPHELES
Bravo, I like to see a burning lover.
The girl is yours in a week or less.
You'll meet her at neighbor Martha's tonight.
A woman expressly made to play the pimp!

FAUST
Good!

MEPHISTOPHELES
But we have to do something for her.

FAUST
One turn deserves another.

MEPHISTOPHELES
We simply have to prove to the law
That her husband's buried in Padua.

FAUST
Very smart! So now we go to Padua?

MEPHISTOPHELES
Holy stupidity! Of course not;
That's a waste of time; we'll swear it's so.

FAUST
If that's your best thinking, count me out!

MPEHISTOPHELES
What, a saint? You'll turn over a new leaf?
If this the first time you've given false witness?
Have you not pontificated about God,
Man, the inner motives,
Given definitions, even, with bragging eye?
Come on! Confess you understood as much of that
As where old Swerdtlein's dead and buried.

FAUST
Still the lying Sophist!

MEPHISTOPHELES
I a liar? Don't you plan
To flatter and seduce Margareta,
To swear you love her as your soul?

FAUST
With all my heart!

MEPHISTOPHELES
How splendid!
Doubtless, you'll swear undying love,
Talk of love's unqiue privilege to overrule the law,
Fantastic, what the human mind produces.

FAUST
But it's true if I can hold the spirit!

I may not find the right words,
I want to express the living flame!
I hurl my senses and intuition through Creation
To find the sacred speech
And I do call this passion eternal, undying!
Where is the sophistry in that?

MEPHISTOPHELES
You see, I was right.

FAUST
From now on, I won't waste my breath.
Repeat yourself enough, you'll seem right.
I've had my fill of your insistence,
And agree with you out of that necessity.

Scene 10

(Garden. Margareta on Faust's arm. Martha and Mephistopheles walk up and down.)

MARGARETA
I feel as if you're condescending to me;
And so you shame me by demeaning yourself.
Travellers learn to be content with very little.
I know I don't have much to say
To such an experienced man.

FAUST
A single look or word of yours is worth more
Than all the cleverness on earth. *(Kisses her hand.)*

MARGARETA
Please! My hands are ugly and rough!
I have to scour and scrub and polish!

And my mother gives me very little money!

MARTHA
And so you're always travelling?

MEPHISTOPHELES
Yes, business and duty drive us to it.
It's even sad to find a beautiful city,
Since one knows one has to leave it.

MARTHA
Oh, when you're young and full of oats, fire!
Careening around the world seems gay.
But luck changes, bad times come, and age.
And an old bachelor creeping
Lonely to his grave is a pathetic sight.

MEPHISTOPHELES
I shudder when I look at fate!

MARTHA
Take warning before it's too late.

MARGARETA
You're easy with your courtesy,
But out of sight is out of mind!
You have many friends more clever than I.

FAUST
Dear girl, don't be deceived;
So-called cleverness is usually vanity or specialism.

MARGARETA
How so?

FAUST
True souls hardly ever guess their real value;

Unaffected love is Nature's highest grace.

MARGARETA

Think for an hour about me sometime!
I have all the time to think on you.

FAUST

You are alone a lot, then?

MARGARETA

Yes. Our household's small,
But there's plenty to do.
We have no maid so I do the knitting,
Sewing, cooking, cleaning, all the errands.
My mother's exact in all the details!
Not that she needs to be so economical;
Our father left us better off than many.
Yet things are slower now –
My brother's a soldier,
And my little sister's dead –
Of course, I had to take care of her,
But I adored her so.

FAUST

If she was like you, of course!

MARGARETA

I raised her and she loved me.
She was born after my father died.
My mother was so ill she could not feed her,
And so I nursed it with milk and water.
Laying on my lap, it seemed mine,
I sang to it, and it prospered.

FAUST

You knew the purest human happiness.

MARGARETA
Also many anxious hours.
I kept its cradle near my bed at night,
And if it stirred, I'd nurse or hold it.
If still it cried, I'd dandle it
And walk about the room.
Then early in the morning,
At the washtub, then marketing,
Then cooking, the same old round.
That way, one's spirits are not always high,
But food tastes good, and rest's pure delight.

MARTHA
It's not easy for us poor women
To convert a confirmed bachelor.

MEPHISTOPHELES
Then someone like you
Must show me the light.

MARTHA
Hasn't anyone ever been special in your life?

MEPHISTOPHELES
The proverb tells me
That home and wife are gold and jewels.

MARTHA
But have you never felt the desire?

MEPHISTOPHELES
I've always been well entertained.

MARTHA
But you've never been touched in earnest?

MEPHISTOPHELES
I've learned never to jest with women.

MARTHA
You don't understand me!

MEPHISTOPHELES
I understand that you are very kind.

FAUST
You knew that we had met before,
You recognized me at the garden gate, didn't you?

MARGARETA
You knew that when I dropped my eyes.

FAUST
And you forgive me for accosting you?
My freedom in taking your arm?

MARGARETA
I was confused; this had never happened to me.
Nothing could ever have been spoken against me,
But your daring made me think
My conduct might be a little loose;
You seemed to take me all for granted.
But I confess something in me liked you.
I grew angry with myself
That I couldn't be angrier with you!

FAUST
You darling!

MARGARETA
Wait awhile. *(Plucks flower. Picks petals.)*

FAUST
Making a daisy-chain?

MARGARETA
It's only a game.

FAUST
What kind?

MARGARETA
You'll laugh at me. *(Murmurs)*

FAUST
What are you whispering?

MARGARETA
He loves me – he loves me not –

FAUST
Sweet girl!

MARGARETA
He-loves-me-not, he-loves-me!

FAUST
Yes, my girl, truth talks to you through flowers!
He loves you!
What does that mean to you? He loves you!

MARGARETA
I'm afraid!

FAUST
Don't be. Look in my eyes.
Hold my hands.
Let them talk to you beyond words.
Ah, love, to completely yield oneself,
To yield and feel eternal bliss!
Eternal! Because if this ends,
Despair is all. No, no ending, no ending!
(Margareta clasps his hand, then runs from him.)

MARTHA
The night's falling.

MEPHISTOPHELES
Yes, we must go.

MARTHA
I'd gladly ask you to stay,
But there's so much gossip here.
You'd think they had nothing else to do,
But spy upon their neighbors.
You're talked about no matter what you do.
But where's our couple now?

MEPHISTOPHELES
Flown up the garden path like butterflies.

MARTHA
He seems to like the girl.

MEPHISTOPHELES
And she likes him. That makes the world go round.

Scene 11

(The garden summer house.)

MARGARETA
He's coming.

FAUST
So now you're teasing me?
I've caught you now. *(Kisses her.)*

MARGARETA
Dear man, I love you with all my heart.

FAUST
Who's there?

MEPHISTOPHELES
A friend.

FAUST
A lout!

MEPHISTOPHELES
It's time for you to leave.

MARTHA
Yes, sir, it's late.

FAUST
Can I take you home?

MARGARETA
My mother would – goodbye!

FAUST
I can't stay? Goodbye.

MARTHA
Adieu.

MARGARETA
Till we meet again, soon!
(Faust and Mephistopheles leave.)
How can a man think so well,
Know so much?
I stand tongue-tied,
And all I can say is Yes.
An ignorant child –
I don't know what he sees in me.

Scene 12

(Forest and cave.)

FAUST

You have given me all that I prayed for,
Sublime spirit.
You revealed Nature's splendid secrets,
And gave me power to hold and enjoy her.
You taught me to seek within her heart,
Trustingly, as I would a friend's.
All living creatures have you linked to me,
From sky and water and forest.
During the roaring storms
You led me to deep caverns
Where, physically secure,
You showed me my own self,
And unfolded secret miracles in my heart.
And when moonlight floats from precipice and thicket,
Myths and phantoms of antiquity rise
To soften thought's austere delight.

But now I see, man's given nothing perfect.
This ecstasy that brings me near the gods,
Ties this comrade to me I can't do without.
His scorn makes me cheap in my own sight;
With a word he destroys all your gifts.
His fire consumes my body;
I never weary of that beautiful girl.
My desire careens to satisfaction.
Satisfied, I crave desire.

MEPHISTOPHELES
(Entering)

Haven't you been in the forest long enough?
You should try everything out,
But then go off to something new.

FAUST

Don't you have something else to do,
Than to disturb such a fine day?

MEPHISTOPHELES

I'd like to let you sit there.
But you don't dare complain for real.
Of course, I'd find losing you a relief,
You're very difficult to please.
No matter how I work,
Your face never gives a clue.

FAUST

That's a fine way for you to talk.
I should give you thanks for boring me?

MEPHISTOPHELES

You wouldn't even be living without my help.
I've at least temporarily
Cleared your clouded brain;
Without me, you'd already have shot yourself.
So why have you slunk off all alone,
To blink your eyes in an owl's cave?
Or drink from moss and stone like a toad?
You're still Herr Doctor, the Professor.

FAUST

You can't know how wilderness uplifts me;
If you could, you'd grudge me that.

MEPHISTOPHELES

Oh, yes, a supernatural delight!
To lie in night and dew on mountains,
To identify with the starry sky,
Ecstatically believe yourself godlike,
To probe with your pulse earth's orogeny,
Pack within your images Creation's six days,

Tasting all that vanity and pride can offer,
Attain love's universal union,
Transcend yourself, then use this new intuition –
(Makes sexual gesture.)
Even I don't like to say to what complexion.

FAUST
For shame!

MEPHISTOPHELES
You're angry, and sudden champion
Of morality, cry for shame in self-applause.
One can never say to chaste ears
What those chaste hearts can't do without.
But, friend, I don't object;
Lie to yourself when it seems profitable.
You're not standing up well to this new life;
You already look a little worn.
If it lasts, madness and horror dawn.
But enough of this! Your little love's lonely,
She can think of nothing but you,
She loves you, how she loves you!
First came your years-repressed passion,
A flood from melting snows,
You unleashed this river, her soul expanded,
But now your water's running out.
Perhaps the great man should leave his posing,
And reward the love of this silly child.
Time drags for her. She haunts the window –
Just looking out. "Were I a bird," she sings.
She sighs, tries to cheer up, cries,
Falls quiet again. She's mad with love.

FAUST
You snake!

MEPHISTOPHELES
I almost trapped you!

FAUST

Why don't you leave?
Don't speak about her again,
Awake desire for her sweet limbs
Once more in my restless senses!

MEPHISTOPHELES

What will you do?
She thinks you ran away, and you did.

FAUST

I can't leave her. She's always here.
I love her so much I'm jealous
When her lips touch the body of her Lord.

MEPHISTOPHELES

I don't doubt it. I've envied you myself
When your lips browsed hers.

FAUST

Pimp! Get out!

MEPHISTOPHELES

Well, I have to laugh even if you rave.
The God who made man and woman
Must have intended procuring opportunity.
Why the moaning and groaning?
You ought to be headed straight for her room.

FAUST

Yes, ecstasy in her arms, peace upon her breast,
But I am her destruction.
I am fickle, homeless, a wanderer,
A monster whose will is like the cataract
That foams down gorges seeking the abyss!
She lived with unawakened sex
In her cottage by the forest.
I not only wish to erode the rocks,

But to undermine her purity,
And sacrifice her to Hell!
Well, devil, let's get it over with.
What must be, let it be right now!
And let me share her fate,
And drag us both to doom!

MEPHISTOPHELES
The passion's on again, it seethes, it glows!
Return, you fool, to comfort her.
Unless you can clearly see the next step
You're the type who thinks the game's up.
I like the steady kind!
Except for this, you're not a bad devil,
But nothing's more insipid
Than a devil in despair.

Scene 13

(Margareta's room.)

MARGARETA
(Alone at her spinning wheel.)
My peace is gone,
My heart is sad,
I'm all alone,
And almost mad.

When he's not here
It's like the grave
There's no cheer,
A dismal cave.

I cannot think
My senses spin

I dream of drink
I cannot win.

My peace is gone
My heart is sad
I'm all alone
And almost mad.

I watch for him,
For him alone.
I go out for him,
For him I moan.

I miss his walk,
I miss his sighs,
I miss his talk,
I miss his eyes.

His magic speech
Became my bliss,
His magic reach,
His magic kiss!

My peace is gone,
My heart is sad,
I'm all alone
And almost mad.

My breast burns
For him alone
My soul yearns
To be his own!

To kiss his face,
To serve desire,
In his embrace,
His kiss, his fire!

Scene 14

(Martha's garden.)

MARGARETA
Promise me, Heinrich!

FAUST
All I can.

MARGARETA
What does religion mean to you?
You're a good man,
But do you worship God?

FAUST
Leave that alone. You know I love you.
Those I love, I'd give my life for.
And I'd take from no man his faith.

MARGARETA
That's not enough. We must believe.

FAUST
Must we?

MARGARETA
I wish I had some influence on you!
You don't honor the Holy Sacraments.

FAUST
I honor them.

MARGARETA
But you have no faith or creed.
How long since you've gone to mass or confession?
Do you believe in God?

FAUST

My dear, who dares say "I believe"?
Ask any priest or truly wise man,
And you will see the answer mocks the asker.

MARGARETA

Then you're an atheist!

FAUST

No, sweet girl, don't take me wrongly.
Who dares puff himself up by saying,
"I believe in God"?
But who with any feeling or insight will say
"I deny God", or "I don't believe in God"?
The Unfathomable, the Source, the Sustainer,
Does he not create, preserve, destroy
You, me, his own creation?
The sky, the stars, the friendly earth,
You and I gazing into each other's eyes,
By these do we not touch the Mysterious Force?
When heaven and earth and love fill your heart,
Call it whatever you wish,
Joy! Heart! Love! God!
I have no name for it.
The certainty's everything,
Names are smoke, blotting out the light.

MARGARETA

All you say is good and very true.
Our priest says the same,
With slightly different words.

FAUST

Every heart beneath the sun cries out the same.
Each from his own time, place and in his words.
Do not blame me for using mine.

MARGARETA
It sounds complete,
But something must be lacking
For you don't seem to have Christ within.

FAUST
Dear girl!

MARGARETA
It makes me sad to see you in such company.

FAUST
Why?

MARGARETA
That man that's with you day and night,
I hate him, Heinrich, with all my soul.
In all my life
I've seen nothing colder than his face.

FAUST
Don't be afraid of him.

MARGARETA
I've wished well for everyone I've met,
But that man's presence makes me ill.
I want to see you more than I can tell you,
But I'm terrified that he will come.
I think he's dishonest through and through!
If I'm wrong – God forgive me.

FAUST
It takes all kinds to make this world.

MARGARETA
I can never live in that man's company!
As soon as he comes inside, he sneers, is angry.

You can see he cares for nothing,
It's written on his face that he hates life and love.
I'm so happy in your arms, free, warm, yielding,
But his presence shrivels me right up.

FAUST
You are full of dread.

MARGARETA
He has such power that as soon as he's here,
I feel even my love for you goes away.
When he's near, I can't say a prayer.
Heinrich, it's the same with you, I know!

FAUST
It's a mere antipathy.

MARGARETA
I must go.

FAUST
Will I never have the chance
To spend a night alone with you,
Lie breast to breast and soul to soul?

MARGARETA
Ah, if I only slept alone,
I'd open the doors for you tonight.
But mother sleeps so lightly,
And if she discovered us, it would mean my death.

FAUST
Don't worry, angel. Here is a vial.
Shake out three drops into her cup.
She'll gently go to sleep.

MARGARETA
I would do anything to please you!

It won't hurt her?

FAUST
If it would, would I advise it?

MARGARETA
Dearest man, you only have to look
And some power compels me to your will.
I've already done so much for you,
There's hardly anything left to do. *(Leaves)*

MEPHISTOPHELES
(Enters)
Your little girl has left?

FAUST
Spying again?

MEPHISTOPHELES
Yes, I heard how she drew you out,
Catechized the learned Doctor,
Girls always like to see religion honored.
If he bends his head there, they think,
They can lead him by the nose.

FAUST
You monster, you can't see or admit
That this true and loving girl,
Filled with a faith which she believes
The only promise of spiritual life,
Tortures herself with the fear
That the man she loves so much is lost.

MEPHISTOPHELES
You supersensual sensualist,
Your desire lets a little girl lead you by the hand.

FAUST
Abortion of fire and filth!

MEPHISTOPHELES
And she reads faces like a book!
When I'm near – she shudders.
She smells out something,
That behind my mask's a hidden purpose,
Maybe even the devil's force.
And so – tonight?

FAUST
What's that to you?

MEPHISTOPHELES
Oh, I get some pleasure from that, too!

Scene 15

(At the well. Margareta and Lisbeth with pitchers.)

LISBETH
Have you heard about Barbara?

MARGARETA
No. I don't go out much.

LISBETH
Well, it's true, Sybil told me today,
She's played the fool, it can't be hidden,
And she put on such airs!

MARGARETA
How?

LISBETH
When she eats and drinks, she's feeding two.

MARGARETA
Poor girl!

LISBETH
It serves her right.
She clung to him, wouldn't let him go.
Promenaded, danced, played high-and-mighty.
She shone at the fair and dances,
He brought her the best wine and pastries,
She never turned down a present.
Oh, they cooed, caressed and kissed,
And now her blossom's gone!

MARGARETA
The poor, poor girl.

LISBETH
You feel sorry for her?
The likes of us spun and cooked,
Our mothers kept us in at night,
She was at it with her lover
On the bench, the porch, in the park,
They never cared how much time they spent.
But now the story's finished, she'll repent,
Stand exposed in the Church with her white sinner's gown!

MARGARETA
He'll surely marry her.

LISBETH
He'd be a fool.
A bright young man finds other girls.
He's already gone.

MARGARETA
That's not fair!

LISBETH
And if by accident she does get him,
We'll make her sorry.
The boys will snatch her wreath, we'll throw chaff!
(Leaves)

MARGARETA
How I used to scorn seduced girls!
How my tongue censured their weakness!
Black as it could be, I made it blacker,
If I could have found words blacker still.
I thanked my fate, paraded virtuously,
Now I face Lisbeth's shame with the same sin.
Yet all that drove me to it
Seemed so good, so sweet, so true!

Scene 16

(Street by Margareta's house.)

VALENTINE
I've sat in many drinking parties,
The kind where each man's allowed his brag,
Each man drank to the honor of his girl.
I'd listen, propped on my elbows,
Stroking my beard; I'd rise, the last one,
Raise high my chock-full mug and say,
"Each girl is good enough in her own way,
But where is one like Greta?
Who can hold a candle to her?"
"Hear, hear!" And always some would add, "How true!"
The ones who feared they lied fell silent.
But now I could tear my beard out!

Any innuendo may be aimed at me,
Any scoundrel could sneer at me,
And though I'd fight anyone who said a word,
I couldn't call him a liar!
Who's sneaking over there? Two of them.
If *he's* one, he won't leave here alive!

FAUST
As the darkness gathers from the sky,
I feel shadow growing in my heart.

MEPHISTOPHELES
Me, I feel like a tomcat on the prowl,
Climbing fire escapes and padding over walls,
But moral, too, not too greedy nor too lecherous.
I feel anticipation for our great Walpurgis Night,
It's only two nights off,
That night nobody regrets his loss of sleep!

FAUST
And the treasure will be seen?

MEPHISTOPHELES
You yourself can lift the cauldron.
The last time I saw it,
It overflowed with gold sovereigns.

FAUST
At least one bracelet for Margareta!

MEPHISTOPHELES
I do remember a string of pearls.

FAUST
Good! I always like to take her a present.

MEPHISTOPHELES
You should learn to take your enjoyment free!

Meanwhile I'll sing you a masterpiece,
A moral song, the better to cheat her later.
Katie, dear,
Why're you here,
Sunrise is near,
Before your lover's door.

He lets you in,
Your love to win,
Your heart will sin,
You leave a maid no more.

He's on the make,
He will take,
Then he'll shake
You off, poor thing!

When love is hot
Don't trust the lot,
Keep what you've got,
Until he gives the ring!

VALENTINE
Who're you trying to seduce, rat-catcher!
First, I'll smash your guitar, then you!

MEPHISTOPHELES
You've ruined the guitar.

VALENTINE
And now your head.

MEPHISTOPHELES
Be bold, Professor, don't run away.
Stick close to me. Out with your spit –
Now you thrust and I will parry.

VALENTINE
Then parry that!

MEPHISTOPHELES
Of course!

VALENTINE
That too!

MEPHISTOPHELES
Easily!

VALENTINE
You're fighting like the devil!
Hey! What's this? My hand's withering!

MPEHISTOPHELES
Thrust home!

VALENTINE
O God! *(Falls)*

MEPHISTOPHELES
That tames the mad dog.
Let's get away! They'll cry *Murder!*
The police I could fix, the Court I'm not sure.
(They leave.)

MARTHA
(Enters)
Neighbors! Come out! *(Margareta and crowd enter.)*

MARGARETA
Bring a light!

MARTHA
There's been yelling and a fight!

CROWD
Here's one already dead!

MARTHA
Which way did the murderers go?

MARGARETA
Who's lying there?

CROWD
Your mother's son.

MARGARETA
No. No! Valentine!

VALENTINE
I'm dying! Easy said, easier done!
Shut up, you moaning women.
I want you to hear my last words!
You're young and not too bright,
Or you'd pay more attention to your business.
Since you're a whore, you ought to work full time.

MARGARETA
Brother! God! How can you give me such a name?

VALENTINE
Leave God out of this filthy game!
What's done's done; now the consequences.
You start with one, others come,
After a dozen, the whole town knows you.
Shame is born in secret delight,
Then she walks veiled at night,
Grown stronger, she strolls in broad daylight,
Though she's none the prettier for that.
The uglier, the more she puts on a show,
Shame always finishes shameless!
Soon any honest person will turn from you,

You whore, as from an infected corpse.
You'll shiver, guilty, when they stare at you.
They'll not let you near the altar.
You can't make merry at the dances.
You'll live with beggars, the crippled, the diseased.
God may forgive your evil,
But here, man has damned you forever!

MARTHA
You should be asking pardon!
You spend your last seconds in blasphemy!

VALENTINE
You pimping female!
If I had strength to reach and kill you,
Then I'd hope for grace to save me!

MARGARETA
Brother! *This* is the pain of Hell!

VALENTINE
Stop your crying! When you gave up your honor,
That's what stabbed me to the death.
Now to solemn death I go;
An honest soldier, God, accept me so.

Scene 17

(Walpurgis Night in Harz Mountains.)

MEPHISTOPHELES
We're still a long ways off. Tired of walking?
Wouldn't you like a devilish machine to carry you?

FAUST
As long as my legs hold out,

My walking stick's enough.
What do we gain by shortening our journey?
I love to hike through the valleys,
Climb the cliffs toward waterfalls,
This gives the zest to travelling!
Spring's quivering in the firs and birches,
How can my legs not feel it?

MEPHISTOPHELES
Well, this marvel doesn't stir in me.
Winter still rules my body,
And I expect snow and ice at any minute.
The moon's so dim we're bumping into branches.
I'm going to call a will-o'-the-wisp.
There's one! Ho, my friend, will you come here?
Don't waste your light, show us the way.

WILL-O-THE-WISP
I hope respect will help my temperament –
Usually we only go zig-zag.

MEPHISTOPHELES
Imitating people?
Well, in the Devil's name go straight,
Or I'll blow your candle out.

WILL-O-THE-WISP
The Master demands his recognition,
And cheerfully I'll do my best,
But today the mountain's magic,
And if you take Will-o'-the-wisp as guide,
He can't guarantee perfection!

TRIO CHANTS
Now we enter dreams.
Do your duty, guide!
Tree after tree glides by,
Cliffs frown, gulches roar!

Brooks pour downward!
Lovers' voices! Sounds of hope!
Exultation! Lamentations!
Echoes like old traditions!
Hoo-hoo, Shoo-hoo!
Screech-owl, jay and dove
Lizards in the bushes.
Roots reach out like octopi.
Rats and mice along the path!
Are we stopped or advancing?
All is whirling, merging, dancing,
The forest's full of faces,
The wild-fire's insane grimaces!

MEPHISTOPHELES
Grab my coat and hold on tight!
Now on this peak see Mammon's blaze!

FAUST
Yes, that rocky cliff seems all on fire!

MEPHISTOPHELES
Mammon can always afford to light his palace.
You are lucky to see the sight,
But now I smell his guest!

FAUST
The storm's howling and whistling!

MEPHISTOPHELES
Hold onto the rock or it'll blow you off!
The night's black with mist.
Listen to the trees crack and crash!
To the owls shrieking!
The boughs moan, the roots strain,
The trunk breaks, and the tree-top falls.
Over the littered gorges, the pitiless wind!

Now you can hear the voices.
Through the mountains pours their song.
Glamorous, magic, maddening, furious!

WITCHES

We witches ride to Brocken's top,
Over golden stubble and the green green crop;
The crowd comes here for lots of fun,
And the Devil's sure to see it done;
Over the valleys we speed along,
Our he-goats stinking, our farts our song!

VOICE

Here sails old Baubo now
Astride her fat old farrow sow!

WITCHES

Then honor be to whom honor's due,
Dame Baubo forward! And lead our crew!
With a pregnant sow and eyes pell-mell
She can take us here or straight to Hell!

VOICE

Which way did you come?

VOICE

By Ilsestein.
I peered right into the nest of an owl.
Did it glare and shriek and howl!

VOICE

Why in the name of Hell go so fast?

WITCHES

This way is wide, this way is long,
Why such a crowded crazy throng?
The brooms scratch, the pitchforks poke,

The womb may split, the infant choke.

WARLOCKS

We crawl along like a snail in a shell
The women ahead with a powerful spell;
When to the Devil we start our races,
Women have an edge of a thousand paces.

We do not moan and wail
That women lead, we bring up the tail;
Let them hurry, let them thump,
Man gets there with one good jump!

VOICE

Come on, you down there by the lake!

VOICES

We'd like to fly with you!
We wash and wash to clean ourselves,
But we stay earthbound and sterile!

WITCHES & WARLOCKS

The wind grows quiet, the stars grow pale,
The moonlight begins to fail;
Fire! Fire! Sparks of fire!
See us witches careen and gyre!

VOICE

Stop! Stop! Ho!

VOICE

Who calls from down there in that canyon?

VOICE

Take me along with you, take me!
I've climbed for three hundred years,
I've never found the magic crag,

Among my sisters I want to jag!

WITCHES & WARLOCKS
He who knows the ancient rotes
Can fly on brooms and goats;
He who can't fly tonight,
Has no hope in his ignorant plight!

VOICE
I try to climb, but my feet are sore,
At home misery; and here no more.

WITCHES
Here's a hint if you fear you'll fail,
Any rag will do for a sail;
Any plank will wing the sky;
If you can't tonight, you'll never fly!

WITCHES & WARLOCKS
First we sail around the summit
Then land on the ground and begin to drum it!
Brocken shall be crowded far and wide,
Witchery and magic on every side!

MEPHISTOPHELES
They shove and push, scream and chatter!
Spin, whiz, bounce, whistle and clatter!
Flame and fart and speed,
The witches' wordless creed!

Stay near me! Where are you?

FAUST
Here!

MEPHISTOPHELES
So faraway? I must use my power!
Make way, the Tempter comes. Make way!

Professor, hold on, and we'll escape.
This party's wild even for me.
Besides, there's a curious sparkle in the forest.
Let's find out what it is.
Duck in these bushes. We're out of sight!

FAUST
You are contradictorily perverse.
And what a brilliant bit of planning!
We climb Brocken on Walpurgis Night
And then go off to be alone.

MEPHISTOPHELES
But look at those peculiar flames!
A merry party's gathered there,
And small groups are where the action's at.

FAUST
I'd rather be up there
With the great bonfires and clouds of smoke.
The Father of Evil drives that crowd
And riddle after riddle would be solved.

MEPHISTOPHELES
And new one after new one take their place.
Let the crowd rave on; we'll take thought.
From the huge world we make little worlds.
I see some young, naked witches,
And old ones who cleverly keep their clothes on.
For my sake, be kind and courteous.
A little effort and we'll have great fun.
Listen! Music! Come on, I insist!
Don't hesitate, I'll introduce you right,
And you'll thank me for it later.
What do you say? And this group's not tiny.
There's a hundred fires along this cliff.
They chatter, cook, drink, dance, make love,

It's hard to beat this scene.

FAUST

Are you going to act the part of warlock or devil?

MEPHISTOPHELES

Usually I go incognito.
But on feast days you should show your Order;
I don't have the Garter, but I have my cloven hoof.
So let's set out on our tour,
I'll pimp, if you play wooer.

HUCKSTER-WITCH

Gentlemen, don't pass by
Without looking at my display!
I have a stock for the rarest tastes.
No object here that has not inflicted pain.
No dagger that's not cut into flesh,
No cup that hasn't poisoned a healthy being,
No jewel that's not seduced a girl,
No sword not used by a traitor,
Or stabbed a strong man in the back.

MEPHISTOPHELES

Girly, your stuff is out of style!
Time never stops, and what's past is past!
Buy novelties. Only novelties sell nowadays.

FAUST

Awh, wow, wow! Goodbye, reason.
This is a party to end all parties.

MEPHISTOPHELES

Everybody's pressing upward!
We think we're pushing, but we're pushed!

FAUST

Hey, who's that?

MEPHISTOPHELES

Lilith.

FAUST

Who?

MEPHISTOPHELES

Adam's first wife. Be careful of her long hair.
It's all that she wears,
And when a young man's snared by that,
He doesn't escape her easily.

FAUST

That pair of witches!
They've danced like crazy and want to rest!

MEPHISTOPHELES

No rest for the wicked tonight!
Another dance! Grab one! Come on! Join the crowd!

FAUST

Once I dreamed a dream,
An apple tree was mine,
I saw two apples gleam;
They tempted me to climb.

YOUNG WITCH

That fruit has tempted men
Since Adam fell to sin;
I'm happy now to row
That I these apples grow.

MEPHISTOPHELES

A dream once came to me;
I saw an old old tree;
It had a wide wide split,
Wide as it was, I leered at it.

OLD WITCH

I kindly salute
The Master with cloven foot.
If you have the right plug ready,
I'll hold the vacuum steady.

MEPHISTOPHELES

Why did you leave that dancing girl,
She sang well, and was the prize of the night!

FAUST

While she sang, a red mouse jumped out of her mouth.

MEPHISTOPHELES

A trifle! If it'd been grey, you could complain.
But don't give up! This night's for love!

FAUST

Then I saw –

MEPHISTOPHELES

What?

FAUST

Look! Do you see that lonely girl?
It seems to hurt her to walk.
She looks like Margareta!

MEPHISTOPHELES

Let her alone! That thought-form's deadly!
That blank look freezes your blood
Until you are turned to stone.
You've heard of the Medusa!

FAUST

Those are the eyes of a murdered girl.
Eyes not closed by a loving hand.

That's the breast Margareta yielded me.
That's the body I enjoyed.

MEPHISTOPHELES
That *is* the witch's projection, you fool!
She lets each man see his own soul's love.

FAUST
What pain, what ecstasy!
I can't tear myself away.
Around her throat's a ring of red,
As thin as a knife-blade!

MEPHISTOPHELES
You're right.
Sometimes she carries her head under her arm.
Perseus lopped it off.
But why do you still want illusions?

Scene 18

(Open country. Overcast.)

FAUST
She's in misery! Despair! She never had an easy life and now she's shut up in prison! That lovely creature called a common criminal, jailed, subjected to torments! It has come to this!

Treacherous, contemptible Spirit! You kept this from me. Now you stand there, your devilish eyes revealing your hate for humanity. You stand there to spite me with your presence. She's delivered up to spirits of evil and, worse, to hard-hearted fault-finding men. You've put me to sleep with common dissipations, conceal from me her growing misery, and leave her alone and helpless to face her grief and ruin.

MEPHISTOPHELES
She's not the first.

FAUST
Dog of Hell! Abomination! Infinite Spirit, turn this snake into a snake crawling on his belly in the dirt before me so I can crush him with my foot! "Not the first!" Misery! Woe! No man can grasp it, why one, but having been one, why more than one being should be so overwhelmed, that the first victim, in her agony of shame, did not atone for all in the sight of the Eternal Forgiver. The anguish of this one being pierces me to the marrow, while you grin wolfishly at the fate of thousands!

MEPHISTOPHELES
So we arrive at the limit of understanding – where man's mind breaks down in angry madness. Why do you bargain with us if you can't live up to the contract? Run away will you, weak stomach? Did I impose myself on you, or you on me?

FAUST
Don't snap your teeth at me! You disgust me.

Mighty Spirit, Glorious One, you who know me body and soul, why am I chained to this criminal comrade, who fattens in mischief and gorges himself on disasters?

MEPHISTOPHELES
Have you finished?

FAUST
Rescue her, or you will pay! I will dreadfully curse you throughout the life of time!

MEPHISTOPHELES
I can't undo the chains of the Avenger, or turn aside his lightning bolts. "Rescue her?" Who ruined her, me or you? You want to reach for the thunderbolts? It's a good thing you miserable

mortals weren't given that power. You're all tyrants; you want to destroy and kill anybody who crosses you.

FAUST
Take me to her. She must be free!

MEPHISTOPHELES
What of the danger to yourself? You are blood-guilty and the town's up in arms. Avenging spirits wait for the murderer to return.

FAUST
You dare call me that? All death and murder in the world attack you, monster! Take me to her, I tell you, and get her out!

MEPHISTOPHELES
I will take you there. But is all the power of heaven and earth entrusted to me? I'll tell you what I can do. I will cloud the jailor's senses. I will make you master of the keys, and you can lead her out with your human hand. I will keep watch; my magic horses will be ready; and I will make your escape. This much is in my power.

FAUST
Let's go!

Scene 19

(Prison)

FAUST
(Before iron door with keys and lamp.)
I had forgotten these horrors,
Man's collective misery, weakness, fury!
This girl shut into a prison,
Whom the highest emotions made criminal!

I'm afraid to meet her face to face.
I must go in; she's to die at sunrise.

MARGARETA

My mother, that whore,
Did me to death,
My father, that miser,
Sucked out my breath.
My sister so fresh
Picked at my flesh.
A bird flew by!
How I need to fly!

FAUST
(Unlocking door.)

She doesn't dream I'm near.

MARGARETA
(Cowering)

They've come! Bitter death is here.

FAUST

I've come to set you free!

MARGARETA

Aren't you human? Pity me!

FAUST
(Unlocking her fetters.)

Careful, you'll wake up the guards!

MARGARETA

Hangman! How can I be in your power?
Who could give you that power over me?
You've come for me at midnight.
Have pity on me, let me live!
Soon the morning chimes will ring,
They'll ring my death.

And I'm so young, so young.
And beautiful and that ruined me.
My lover hung upon me, now he's gone away.
My flower's plucked, the petals thrown aside.
Don't grab me so violently!
What did I ever do to you?
Please listen, I've never done you any wrong!

FAUST
God! What a mess I've made!

MARGARETA
I can't defend myself against you,
But let me nurse my baby first.
I've held it all night through.
They took it from me out of spite,
And claim I killed it – no!
I can't ever be happy again.
The folks made a mean song about me;
I knew an old ballad with the same ending –
Who told them to sing it about me?

FAUST
I love you! Please let me take you away!

MARGARETA
Let's kneel and ask the Saints to help us!
Beneath this floor Hell hisses!
Don't you hear the Accuser judging me?

FAUST
Margareta!

MARGARETA
That was my lover's voice!
I heard him, where is he?
No one can stop me, I'm loose,

I'll run to him and hug him close.
He stood right there, called "Margareta".
In the middle of the Accuser's roar
I heard his sweet voice.

FAUST
I am he!

MARGARETA
You are he! Say it again!
It is you, and my pain's gone,
My fear of the dungeon and the chains.
You've come to save me,
And I am saved!
I see the street again where we met,
And the garden where Martha and I waited for you.

FAUST
Come! Hurry!

MARGARETA
Stay a little while.
I like it here now you're with me.

FAUST
We must go! It's our only hope!
If we delay we're lost!

MARGARETA
What's the matter? Have you forgotten how to kiss?
You've been gone such a short time,
And you can no longer kiss?
Why am I so afraid of holding you,
And you used to kiss me till I almost fainted.
Kiss me, or I'll kiss you!
Your lips are cold!
Where is your love and passion?
Who did this to me? *(She turns away.)*

FAUST
Follow me! Be brave!
I'll love you a thousand times,
But follow me, please!

MARGARETA
Is it really you?

FAUST
It is. But come on!

MARGARETA
You took my chains off.
You hugged me, caressed me.
How could you bring yourself to do it?
Don't you know whom you've set free?

FAUST
Please come! The sky's lightening already!

MARGARETA
My mother I killed. My baby I drowned.
But that was yours as well as mine.
It is you, though that seems strange.
Give me your hand! I'm not dreaming.
Your own dear hand! But it's wet!
Wipe it off! I think that's blood!
God, what have you done?
Put up your sword, please put up your sword!

FAUST
Let the past alone, or you'll break my heart.

MARGARETA
No, I must die, but you must live.
Tomorrow you must prepare the graves.
My mother gets the best place,
Then my brother,

Then me, a little ways off,
But not too far,
And my baby at my breast.
No one else sleeps beside me!
When you used to, that was my joy,
But that's dead and gone,
As if you'd shut me out of all your heart;
I have to force myself to touch you,
And yet, it *is* you, so good and kind, before me.

FAUST
If you feel it is, then please come with me.

MARGARETA
To where?

FAUST
To freedom!

MARGARETA
I can only go to death.
No other path's left open.
You're leaving?
I wish I could come, my love.

FAUST
You can! Be brave! The door's open.

MARGARETA
I have to stay. I have no more hope.
If I flee, they'll hunt me down.
A miserable life, to hide and beg,
Especially with a bad conscience.
To be an exile is sad enough,
And they'd follow and catch me, anyhow.

FAUST
I'd be with you.

MARGARETA

Quick, quick! Rescue the baby!
Go by the ridge along the brook
To the foot-bridge,
And then into the wood
Where the plank's in the pool –
There, it's trying to swim,
It's still struggling, save it, save it!

FAUST

Use your will! One step and you're free!

MARGARETA

If only we were past the hill,
If only we were already past!
My mother sits upon that stone,
An icy hand seizes me!
She sits and shakes her head,
She does not nod to me.
She sleeps so deeply she'll never wake up.
She slept so we could love,
And we did love, and we were happy!

FAUST

Words don't work; I'll carry you off!

MARGARETA

Don't use force on me! I won't stand it!
Get your murderous hands off me.
All I've done, I freely did for love.

FAUST

It's almost sunrise! Margareta!

MARGARETA

Day? Yes, the day, the last day!
My wedding day, it might have been.
Don't tell anyone you were here.

No wedding flowers – too late, now!
We'll meet again, but never at the dance!
The crowd is gathering,
On the square and in the streets.
They toll the death bell.
They tie me, deliver me to the chopping block.
Every neck in the crowd feels the knife near.
The razored steel flashes.
My world disappears!

FAUST
I wish I had never been born!

MEPHISTOPHELES
(Appearing)
You'll be lost, too, if you stay. It's dawn!
This talking and sobbing is useless!
My horses are trembling; let's get out of here!

MARGARETA
Who is this thing?
It's he, it's he!
He wants my soul!
He waits for my death!

FAUST
You shall live!

MARGARETA
I abandon myself to God's judgment!

MEPHISTOPHELES
Come on, or I'll abandon you!

MARGARETA
Father, I am yours! Rescue me!
Heinrich! I'm afraid of you!

MEPHISTOPHELES
She's judged and doomed to die.

VOICE
She shall live!

MEPHISTOPHELES
You, come with me!
(Disappears with Faust.)

MARGARETA
Heinrich! Heinrich!